CODE OF BANKING PRACTICE - really?

Banking Beyond Men and the Orchard of Bad Apples

Warning: The name has nothing to do with a Gender Bias the fact is that Finance in a male dominated industry and it began with Men. Now we need Men and Women to take notice and make the necessary changes needed to prevent further abuse of power within the system.

This **Publication is not the original Code of Practice; it is not advice to be relied upon however it is based on true events and real outcomes.**

The Banker's Association in 2003 made the first publication, still nothing much has been amended to hold the human beings in position of power, accountable for the Financial Abuse driven by EGO and Greed.

Now all you should know and not what others tell you are explained and not sugar coated. Don't sign anything again without knowing the Ugly Truth. Never be afraid to stand up for your own LIFE. There is HOPE even when you are declared voiceless.

Depicted from the actual Code of Practice. **No offence to anyone in the Banking Sector.** It contradicts the guidelines that have been written with the actual actions of the employee and how they get away with the unthinkable.

It is what it is and no businesses of this magnitude can manage the human behaviour of their staff, especially when they too are but a number in the scheme of things.

We are dealing with toffee apples; rotten apples coated and camouflaged by the system.

After years of dealing with not only my own battles within the Banking System, I have dedicated years in many battles alongside the Voiceless Victims who have been abused by people in positions of power (PPP System of Abuser)

Table of Contents

INTRODUCTION

For centuries men have dictated and set up our financial futures and after everything that continues to reoccur with Banking (finance), perception of property value, the economy, and basically our lives, it was time to face the Ugly Truth. We are responsible for our own lives!

Who am I to tell anyone about this subject? I am a person that has survived all forms of abuse and then continued to help others (with successful outcomes) after they were already destitute. Been There, Done That and NOT Letting it Continue!

My Life has come full circle as I had explained in my first book. 'The Heart of Hope!' After completing much more than I could ever imagine, it was time to allow others to know my story. Yes, we all have one, I know, and mine is just one of many when it came to Abuse and creating a new life against the odds. I guess I waited until I actually did it and came out the other end before I could assist others. There was nothing that another person could inflict that I hadn't survived before, and so I managed to guide many who had suffered at the hands of another human being.

Basically, in a more condensed version, I am a single mother, a multi-passionate-female that has spent 30 years in Male dominated industries. My experience and expertise in Trouble shooting and innovative concepts has lead to my current role as an Advocate for Fairness in the Banking sector. Having mediated with very reputable Law Firms and various Banking institutions with successful outcomes for all concerned.

I have bought and sold properties that I worked hard to purchase and, ultimately during my life, I encountered many situations where I had to learn and implement quickly … coming up against "professionals." For example; Colourful accountants, brokers and bankers, legal representatives used strategically to protect the perpetrator and discredit the victim. Receivers and Liquidators, all with personal agendas used to ensure the customer loses control in order to protect the creditor (Bank) and discredit the victim. Unfortunately the systems we have are still in place allowing the abuse to continue to date. My Attitude is not to allow others to go through the same abuse and manipulation, having been there, done that. I became an advocate (the technical term apparently) at giving a voice to the voiceless.

This is not a Book or a spiel to SELF HELP or to get onto the Motivational Treadmill. There are already so many, it is confusing because everyone is promoting how to become something and do such amazing things with your life, whatever...

You are 'Enough', just as you are, we only need to be aware of the hidden Abuse when it comes to Money. It's great when it's going right but is debilitating when it all goes wrong we find ourselves stuck and reliant on a professional that really isn't in your shoes.

We are all experts at something except when it goes wrong xo.

This book is to expose the Bad Apples and the ugly truth about LIFE. Things the system does best as it continues to inflict financial and emotional abuse that has led to violence. Yet we have been helpless in defending ourselves. My LIFE started in a very controlling and abusive environment, and I came out the other end without support. I continued to witness, defend, and overcome the greatest monsters in various industries. Surviving the GFC (General Finance Culture; my own personal definition) and defending myself against professionals who held a position of power. These internal abusers consider themselves protected species. I'd over came my own injustices and clearly winning by saving my assets and losing in other areas, because I had other lessons to discover.

The wolves I was surrounded by, all dressed in

sheep's clothing, abused my personal trust making me susceptible to their manipulation. We give our trust so easily to strangers with a piece of paper that states that basically they paid money to go to University, so they must be somehow more qualified and better than you.

Bad Apples can be hidden amongst a large crop until they decay and start to smell. Over the last decade, all I have done with my time is fight for fairness and justice, problem solving in different industries with results.

Before you make a judgment, I am multi-passionate-preneur … meaning I am passionate about a few different projects. They are Construction and the Environment (utilisation of Flyash and manufacturing environmentally friendly concrete solution), a Transport Solution for Sydney and the reason I have stepped up on a Vulnerability Platform is Diva Enterprises. Diva Enterprise is a holistic solutions community that will Educate to Empower & Eradicate Abuse & provide choices.

A Very diversified Woman is the only way I can explain myself without sounding scattered.

How I got to this point was a **"destined to do so,"** situation in my life.

After having saved myself and assisting a number of people by advising on what I knew, the ugly truth, and what their rights were (no, I am not a lawyer), they would consult with me and together we achieved resolution from Banks mainly. Having also dealt with and worked for receivers and liquidators, I also got to understand the world of business and how important it was to set up your business correctly. This saw me dealing with ASIC, ATO, and various other regulatory bodies in New South Wales and Queensland. I was a female in a man's world of dominance, and because I did not have that piece of paper (license to dictate) it made it very challenging. Without a CV (certified victimization) that stated what degree I'd completed it automatically insinuated the other person was the smart one. I had to prove myself more times than I care to recall. No offence to anyone, but it can be very daunting and LIFE happens so you may not have had a choice in your academia.

Having come up against lawyers who represent the Banks, to CEOs, and management of their various divisions, I would always have the voiceless victim present so he or she ultimately made their own decisions. There are many situations that have been resolved and not publicized. So as far as I was concerned my University degrees in an illogical way, were paid with personal currency that consumed my existence, somehow more costly than a debt to the government for Fee Assistance.

Every situation differed, but was ultimately the same outcome; those decisions that were made had been overturned. All this was great; apart from the fact the emotional element remained violated even after the acknowledgement of misconduct. The settlement somehow made the abuse more evident. The pain was so real, though the relief and tears of gratitude were concealing a mixture of emotions that were never dealt with as the battle and burden of proof lingered. Having your entire life destroyed with a stroke of a pen is torturous when you are left bewildered and then questioning how the situation ever came to be?

It's almost like drinking with a trusted friend and you become intoxicated within his environment. You trust that you are in safe hands and then in the morning you experience the worst hangover as your memory becomes vague ... what just happened? You question your every move, your every conversation, as you discover this trusting person had violated you. He was no gentleman; he had no integrity and he concealed his true motives as he led you to your self- destruction. It's really that bad and there is no nice way of putting it or teaching it. Guys, it's the same for you in many cases, except it damages your ego and ability to provide for your loved ones, it's the same hurt and betrayal.

Money is one word that some fear, others yearn for or avoid, and some love. It brings out the worst and best in people; it creates wars and dictates poverty. Ultimately, it can also discriminate. So far I have worked on a number of varying stories where the banker has taken advantage of the customer by using his position of power to manipulate and benefit him and others. The results speak for themselves. Now we all need really to listen to the words we read because although you may believe it will **never** happen to you, one day it just might, given that the actions we are endorsing are a cycle. It all comes around full circle and we should be prepared, especially when we have observed, experienced, and overcome the booms (explosions) and bubbles (false economy) many times over. History keeps repeating.

We are witnessing and hearing many more allegations of corrupt behaviour amongst our professional bodies, the ones that had turned a blind eye in previous years. How many more enquiries and how much more is yet to come to light?

"Lies have short legs, they can't run very far." MC

1. So we begin …

We have all heard of or know someone to whom things happened and then they decide to put their experience into good use. It happens daily, just look on any social media platform! This book came about because after a long battle with Goliath (The Banks), I literally had enough! The numerous complaints made and ignored by many, the enquiries that accept the well-scripted responses of denial and arrogance by management, and the politics behind the acceptance of these actions.

There is no other reason except finally to state the ugly truth that many continue to cover up and to find excuses for ruining lives. We are dealing with human nature, after all, not all humans use their position of power to manipulate the systems to feed their egos and lifestyles. However there are a number of Bad Apples!

Having placed myself on the vulnerability stage with my own LIFE story, The Heart of Hope, it made no sense to keep quiet.

For the last 4 years, I have been quietly achieving results for many who had become voiceless. A Voice for the Voiceless! I know, I already said this! These families were all made Bankrupt and lost not only their ability to be heard but also the ability to rebuild and most importantly their identity.

Having faced my own personal issues with 2 major banks in Australia, one of the big four and the other was a franchise, where the managers (owners) had to meet their quota set by their head office. During 2008 (when the GFC hit) I found myself in a helpless situation when my home and investment assets were being defaulted by the Bank (one of the Big Four). The banker had to pass the file on to her supervisor, a man that I met on several occasions. I'll call him Pete in this instance; he had previously been overly friendly and very inquisitive about the asset I had purchased and renovated. This created a passive income of significance which that also paid for the mortgage on the home. He labeled it a 'cash cow'; I called it my 'MMPV (More Money Purpose Vehicle), I gave everything in my world a meaning at that stage. Given that at the time of this purchase and plan, I had been passing on valuable projects such as this one to my employer. This time I took the leap of possibility (LOP) and did it for me!

Now Pete was a friendly but cunning man, to say the least, nevertheless he couldn't just take over the file. *"There were procedures."*

Each department has a specific functionality. At the time, my investment was held in a family trust, as this was also my retirement and given I had finally

—

set a secure foundation I was now able to plan for the future and my security as I grew old. Being a single mother and realising that Prince Charming was not coming on his white horse any time soon, I viewed this as my superannuation and was conscious on protecting it and managing it properly. During this time I admit I had a financial mentor (a colleague that I usually passed on these 'cash cows' this time I had done it for myself!) although he was a little disappointed, he gave me 'free' advise and offered support. Together with my then banker, she and I discussed all that could be done and I made certain I didn't accept anything that would jeopardize the asset. I was on a low margin and interest rate which was locked in for a period of 10 years. This was unheard of, apparently, but was done; to date, I never found out if my relationship banker was reprimanded for working with me and not against me.

At the time I had other businesses and also referred a number of people to the Bank, who appeared to be doing the right thing by me now. My Loan to Value Ratio was great and my Asset was an income-producing Asset that made it a 'No Brainer' so I pushed for this security and insisted on a 'better deal' given that my investment property was lucrative.

> *"You can do a great deal with the Banks if you speak up and not just settle for their 'only' options."(Diva Tip)*

So, the next thing that happened during the 2008 GFC panic, in November of that year, I received a notice that interest rates were varied on another facility (equipment lease).Somehow this resulted in another notice stating that my facility had expired and the file was being moved away from my banker to Pete. She (my banker) had no say in the matter, apparently. Pete was friendly enough and knew the entire file and situation; surely he would be able to get to the bottom of this? My facility was fixed and there was no way it had expired! Just not possible!

He knew this so I had nothing to worry about – even he said so!

WRONG!

Ultimately it was he that instigated the entire situation.

A Bank can change its mind on your facility and you allow them to, once you sign the agreement. It's camouflaged with all the other strategically placed legal language and never clearly explained to you pre or post execution. They didn't want my 'Risk

Factor' anymore, so I was wasting my breath, even though my asset was income producing and had loads of equity. They didn't lose their appetite they were just 'glutens' I had something that would benefit someone else. That was how simple it was and we have no recourse for this action because the documents allows the Banker to instigate this action without investigation (reality check)

I was called into a meeting at the head office in Sydney, NSW, for a get together to discuss moving forward and here I was to propose how I would rectify the situation … except that was not what the get together was …it was a totally different agenda.

Sitting in the foyer of this elaborate set up, I was asked if there was anyone accompanying me, No ... Me, myself and I that was it! When I walked into the boardroom, I had a suit brigade all sitting around one side of the wall as I sat to face the Spanish Inquisition. That is at least how it felt sitting in an isolated spot around a table that sat 12. After the formalities and all the other nonsensical chatter, someone finally had the guts to ask, "How do you propose to repay your facility with us?"

What The Fairy floss?

First, I was invited here to discuss the situation that had me perplexed, seeking an explanation and the opportunity to work through my options. But I didn't have any...their agenda was different! No one had ever said the bank wanted me to repay the entire facilities and to move banks or worse, sell up! I had been loyal to this bank for as long as I could remember ... Even after the first experience when I was with my ex- keeper who colluded with the banker that allowed him to have even more control over my LIFE...(I was named on a home/construction loan, but never on the title of the home and no income to justify the loan application, no authority on the bank account, however had all the responsibility, how that worked I had no idea...If only I knew what I know now!)

The bank came after me when my ex defaulted (purposely) which was during the time I left with the police, after another episode of violent attacks. I was not on title and had no rights back then and to get back at me he used the bank. *(Now Diva has the programs to stop this happening to others)* When the home was sold, the banks gave him the balance even after knowing of the volatile circumstances and pending family court matter. They ignoring me, however if the house were sold for less than the loan amount, then the bank would not have ignored me. Meaning that I was on that agreement and a guarantor so they'd chase me for the shortfall, no matter what my situation!

Anyhow, I digress. Being loyal meant nothing more that becoming more vulnerable and dependent on the actions of the banker and the internal banking system.

This meeting was one sided, I was not prepared, and had not consulted with a professional of any caliber; deeds of something or other were thrown across the table and accusations without evidence voiced. I didn't default, I had always notified my banker of every financial decision and I never had more debt than asset equity. I simply advised these gentlemen that I would have to get back to them given I was caught off guard. This attempt to ambush and be coerced into something I had no comprehension of was bad enough and I was not going to react emotionally. (An easy thing to do) In the first instance, I am not a lawyer, didn't have representation and didn't need to listen to their elongated reciting of their rights and capabilities. The underlining threats of what the system will do to me meant I definitely did not need to agree to anything at this gathering of men in suits. Regardless that I was terrified internally, I held myself together and politely walked out with the only possible reason being, I will get a lawyer (Another professional because they saw me as a vulnerable female) especially after their commentary and intelligent observation that I was a single mother and would fall apart when they said 'we know you have a young family, that this is difficult!'

That afternoon I went back home and not to work, as I called everyone and anyone with better knowledge than I of the position I faced. Everyone I spoke to advised that I had no options. Like Hell I had no choice, I had been there before, living in a situation where others dictate how you live and that was not where I was going to return.

We all tend to panic and feel helpless given that the Bankers and all people in power portray superiority and invincibility in some aspects. Especially when you have been lead to believe that, 'everything is fine', by your friendly banker so your concern about the unknown is mixed with the emotion of betrayal and disbelief.

We all turn to what we know.... the lawyers who charged for information that would lead you fighting it out in court, but the smart thing to do was just accept the banks demands ...great advice (NOT)! Advisors requested money up front because they estimated a percentage on success and an hourly rate that gave no guarantee. As I discovered, they gave no real support and ultimately it all came back to having a lawyer represent you! Then there was the longstanding advice to declare bankruptcy

---

and go to a 'friendly' liquidator!

There are so many cases where people have declared Bankruptcy when they clearly shouldn't have; this is another decision that is usually made from a concoction of emotional additives! (Poor advice at a vulnerable time)

The free services confused the situation even further because they all contradicted each other and had limitations. My file or compensation was over the threshold of FOS (Financial Ombudsman Service) and others basically said the Banks were well within their rights – there was nothing more they could do!! What Now?

Take responsibility and become my own HERO – Honest Ethical Resourceful Options

That night I remember not going to bed until I had read every document I had, the entire facilities, borrower's copy, and guarantor's version, too. It took me longer to finally get it because I was not *ed-u-macated* and would revert to a legal dictionary and the various policies and stuff I had to research. That night, I don't think I slept as I went from room to room to check on all the children. My mother had passed away just prior to this happening; in 2008. Thank God she didn't witness all this..

Early that morning, I sent through another complaint to FOS (Financial Ombudsman Service). You see, I made a complaint about the facility being locked in for years then having been told that I defaulted due to expiration. But also the fact that I was tricked into this meeting without representation was worse, what were they thinking? The initial complaint should have stopped any action from occurring, but it didn't and it was explained that the bank had not been notified prior to this meeting. This was their explanation to excuse the actions of the bankers and avoid further accusations of wrongdoing and bullying given by the men in power, at this get together.

"No discrimination meant in that statement, only an observation, that it has always been mainly Males in these roles. Now we see more females but not many in these situations as they are mainly now placed at the head of Infested Orchards to conceal the Bad Apples. Or are they placed in the roles where they are doomed and set to fail and take the fall for the misconduct of others?"

Back to the story; an investigation had commenced, however during 2008 the Ombudsman service (FOS) took forever, (mine took 16 months) they weren't as inundated with complaints as they are now, or perhaps they were? Not as many people knew about this 'free' service back then as most paid exorbitant amounts of money for others to defend them or to give them advice. In most cases you'd find that they wasted time and were ultimately better off seeking help through the 'free' advisory services.

It was during this time (GFC) that many found themselves in trouble regardless of their situation, some were genuine defaults and hardships and others created by Bad Apples. These were often constructed defaults that were undetected due to the internal systems. Various tactics were used and many were well within their rights accord to the documentation, or were they? We now have even more inquires and media exposure to state otherwise.

It didn't stop there I requested the actual applications of all the facilities and original documents that I filled out in detail after the initial 12 months of the Investment property. The home loan had never been an issue, but was now caught up in the entire mess along with the credit cards and business facility. The banker was always encouraging and supportive, she was also helpful when it came to my insistence on protecting asset as part of a retirement plan, or so I thought.

The documents showed that the properties were set up as individual facilities and not to be collectively securitized. Meaning each loan was secured by the property in question, or so I was lead to believe. Unfortunately she never had the final say, this I discovered much later and she wasn't the Bad Apple. The Bad Apple needed her removed from the file ... a file that had sufficient equity to sustain itself and more. There is a formula that allows the bank to ensure it has enough capital. If only I knew it back then!

It's all in the timing ... including when you make your complaints!

The investigation went for a while and still no one was getting anywhere, especially me that continued to be told that there was a process that needed to be followed. At this point, I moved to another bank and had the rental income transferred to this new bank, anticipating the 'what if's' as I learnt about the extent and rights the Banks actually had! I actually refused to pay anything further until all the default interest charges were explained, as they now proceeded to starve me of funds. They couldn't be properly justified and they were credited back, after the notification to management. I opened another account and moved the payments into a new bank, before they could freeze my accounts. (Which they were allowed to do!)

> *"Through Freedom of Information, you can request this information and it must be produced. (Diva Tip)"*

After review of all my accounts and the few responses by the Bank, it was clear that there were many transactions internally that were unexplainable, and not my doing. These are generally not disclosed and always denied. The bank accepted my offer to mediate, even though FOS had a limitation as to the amount of compensation and what they could actually do.

To a certain degree, they really did not look into the matter properly, as my file later revealed. That was the first disappointment with my own experience with the Regulators.

Although not many people consider this after an ombudsman has made his/her finding known to both parties. **You should do this! (Reality check)**

After almost 2 years of back and forth, conversations, and exchange of evidence, an agreement was made. I saved my assets, reduced the debt significantly, and sought to refinance. There is another challenge when you have been transferred to the Asset Risk department of a bank: Generally no other first tier lender will consider you for credit…I was in the right and that had to stand for something. Right?

WRONG!

"Bank will never make any sort of admission regardless of the settlement, so they are never wrong and you are never right"

"Knowing what you think you know, because others said so, meant there were options you'd never know about."

#FACT #DifficultyByDesign

It was during this time that many things in my personal and business life had changed significantly. I was no longer an 'I' having started a relationship and I was also in a very different situation emotionally. I was introduced to a bank manager of a smaller bank; at this time they were a fairly new player in the game of banking, almost a self-regulated banker/manager/owner of a franchise. It was at this time the person introducing me was also a partner (intimate relationship I mentioned) who convinced me to look for a property in another state and promised the happily ever after.

#Mistake no1- too serious too soon and even though I was older and financially independent did not mean I knew better. (LIFE Happens at any stage)

This banker, a very friendly chap, made a house call (he was the owner!) and proceeded to make me out to appear as though I did not want this supposed fairy tale on offer by a partner. I felt awfully uncomfortable as he and this partner (had no financial contribution or risk attached to anything) made out that he was doing me a favour. (This entailed using my assets, my ability, and my repayments!). He went away convincing 'us' that this was attainable and he would be writing up a multi-million-dollar facility shortly! They would be broken up individually because again I was adamant at keeping my retirement asset separate. Even though this banker knew I could not commit to living in another state and had various unsolved issues, still went ahead and insisted this was doable. To be totally honest I was only interested in refinancing from the Bank that I now completed a win-win agreement. I did not need more debt or another home especially one that was not going to be occupied in any way and was creating someone else's fairytale!

This was a sure thing for the bank given the assets in NSW and my retirement plans were so lucrative! So be wary of Bankers bearing Gift – or debt freely!

After a few more meetings and the whole truth and nothing but, he asked me to sign the document giving him authority to proceed and do his checks before I bothered to proceed to an application.

What happened next in short was complete fraudulent activity and stupidity on my part. We were away on a business EXPO when the bank manager called and said it was urgent for me to sign the application document, because now I was running out of time for the refinance and that purchase. Except now with the purchase I would be penalized for delay in settlement!

More Pressure to add to the emotional rollercoaster of LIFE

Basically, the application was all wrong and filled out by the bank manager. The facility was not as he had explained and written on a note pad.

> *"Make sure you always keep a copy and save everything even if it is scribbled on a serviette. It may matter later!" (Diva Tip)*

The valuation actually stated that the fairy-tale home was less than the value on the front page of the contract; regardless the bank had used the sale price/value. The bank knew that my circumstances were changing and that I would not be earning as I used to, due to the demands of my partner. So, basically, the banker knew that the equity in my original properties (investment) had to be used as security and was the most appealing component of the deal.

So he did not care about the realization value in fine print in order to lend responsibly. (Reality Check)

He also had me sign in front of a third party who was affiliated with the bank. He also forgot to mention the short fall on settlement so I had to find the funds at the last minute! This would cause delays and penalties and if the settlement (for the home loan I should never had been given) didn't go ahead the consequence was costly. Not to mention that all loans were declared and investment loan even my home! He also stated the investment property was separate from the others. Basically he did, as he needed to reach his quota!

"I had a right to actually go after the accountants Personal Indemnity Insurance, but didn't" The bankers associate that did not explain anything!

The next discrepancy was a statement he made upon me signing, 'after the first anniversary (because I didn't have a banking history with them) the interest and principle would change to interest only.' That would help with the repayments because my circumstances were changing. He also knew that I would be paying over $20,000 per month, on my own!! During this time I had another issue in the background, yet to unfold but there never the less. None of what he said happened and I found myself in hardship after just barely surviving the repayments for the first year. That house in another state, (I could hardly enjoy and couldn't lease it out much less live in it), was a debt I did not need and actually jeopardized my assets.

My financial security was now at risk whilst the Bank secured theirs.

Everything the banker had promised and said he denied almost immediately. My situation changed as I said in the beginning (even worse) due to the relationship and after 12 months the file was moved to its Asset Collections department. The tactics used once the file was moved were disgusting; the banking staff at a higher level was so calculating and not helpful at all even though they knew the banker should not have provided the loan (maladministration) given the circumstances and their defense to my dispute. No Hardship was offered and default interest was charged even when they were not allowed to do it! Clearly I had more to learn, except this time I had more anguish to deal with having been in an emotionally tormenting relationship at the time. The Bank did not care and the banker/owner was only concerned with his need to reach target!

A complaint was made however this time for actions that were on another scale all together; the bankers involved were from another banking institution, one of the larger

"BANKS. Many had been moved on due to unethical behavior during the GFC, never proven or persecuted however like usual Bankers were either made redundant or resigned and found employment elsewhere. Sadly there was no mandatory reporting like other places, a banker could act unconscionably and still move into another position. Without the new employer ever discovering their dark side leaving them able to continue their systematic deception."

Regardless, FOS (Financial Ombudsman Service) found the bank did nothing wrong even though the evidence was all there, and considering that whilst a dispute has been raised to FOS, the bank is not allowed to be debt collecting, that is EXACTLY what the Banks did! The Bank placed pressure on me at all time to sell down and repay immediately, even though this was not the position I'd be in if the Banker had not insisted.

The emotional pressure and the pressure to refinance were the lethal cocktails that lead to the manipulation and persuasion the banker used in order to entrap me.

You'd think I know better, I thought I did and I knew what to look for and who to turn to when it all went wrong! I did turn to the organizations that were in place to regulate the actions of the Bank, and then I also appealed to the Bank. Once the asset they encouraged me to purchase, was sold then problem solved…no risk to anyone! So I was lead to believe. WRONG. They had ever right apparently to continue to force me to sell my Home and my asset, even when there was no more risk.

This is when I went along with the system and followed everyone's advice, purposely not fighting the system, but listening to their instructions and where it got me was to lose a lot given that it was at the time housing prices started booming.

I sold that property that never should have been allowed and the bank took the little excess that remained. Having completed renovations to improve the place for market. Not having been reimbursed for it. The complaint continues as the bank engaged in some ruthless tactics as I managed to stay one step ahead and noting all the dealings with everyone. The banks continued to debt collect and took proceeds from a sale to which they were not entitled, even according to FOS who pointed out that the Bank did not have the security over the asset.. As usual they denied any wrongdoing and kept on with their bullying tactics, they did nothing about it! The Bank proceeded to Debt collect on a facility that was now 25% LVR (Loan Value Ratio) and not a threat to their exposure, but a threat to my future given they could do as they wished, regardless of the regulatory organisations we have.

All the rights to force sale and debt collect are provided to the Banks and sadly the law allows it. According to the documents it's your own fault – no matter what! This is the poison used to destroy and is considered legal tender.

FOS considered it too hard to deal with after it was done. Now, with the added proof of what actually happened and the obligation of the bank manager to the franchise, it is crystal clear what happened. During this time the pressure placed on the Franchisee to meet their quota meant 'anything goes' and this Bank has now grown considerably. It's almost a GFC Money grab scenario all over; given the methodology used to increase their loan book it was what many other banks had always done. Today this bank is in the papers for increased profits and now amongst the big 4 in home loans. The employees of other institutions all run this bank; obviously it will end the same!

After reviewing the documents from FOS and its internal file of my matter, it is very clear of the questionable conduct.

How ironic that the staff in the asset collections department tried to bully me into signing a Deed of Forbearance.

This is a document that is not compulsory to sign, especially under duress. You need to be cautious, stop, breathe, and think clearly before signing anything under this type of pressure. The banker is obligated to explain this to you and not threaten you with what it will enforce in order to have you sign. You do have rights! (Reality check)

In this instance, I did not sign a deed of forbearance and remained in some form of control over the sale of assets as to when and how and how much. Once you sign a deed, you are handing over what little rights you have. But beware, I then found another industry wolf that was also a Bad apple, this time in the real estate industry. It is not uncommon that they team up to now form an unsuspecting group of Bad Apples to prosper from your situation.. The sale was forced and the new owner was a client of that very bank. In many cases I have traced back relationships that may appear third party but conceal a much closer relationship or convenient association.

(FACT)

You have a statute of limitation when making a claim against the Bank ... so I'm not leaving it too late. From what I have now discovered if you can show negligence you can argue the limitation. Banks have become reliant on this as the cover up continued throughout 2008, to date. Now with the many inquires and investigations I have overturned events from 8 years ago.

These things happen more often than not! That there is a hidden agenda and it isn't just the Bank it happens in every industry.

What happened next led me into another journey in seeking justice in an area that is so unjust! The irony is that the same Bad Apples appeared within the stories of many that I had assisted in battles years later. Sadly many of these people had already felt the full force of an unjust system that allowed the same rotten apples to do as they had always done. Now after the valuable lessons and decoded terminology of their rights, successfully mediated matters have proven that the answer is to understand what you can do when you are told 'you can't'. An education program for you to protect yourself before you fall victim to the same perpetrators. The usual Bad Apples that have moved from Bank to Bank and continued the systematic tactics and use of the internal systems. Not having been reprimanded for their previous actions they have managed to slip through the system and continue their rein of abuse and power validation. There is no discrimination in Banking, we are all seen as opportunities that people in power violate.

That being said not all people in the Banking industry are abusing their positions. The industry of Money creation will always be an industry of temptation and if we were to be honest, we are dealing with human nature. Good, Bad and Indifferent in all of us! Not all are comfortable or willing to mistreat and deceive another human being.

"Bankers move on from one bank (orchard) to another, with some being moved on by management and others strategically moved from Bank to Bank. All know the system and how far the boundaries could be pushed to avoid detection."

I fell into "helping find solutions" for others. Without any monetary gain, I gave my time gratis and now after all the resolved matters (after being told it was impossible!) it has driven me to stand up to a mammoth business (Banking). Creating a niche business model that will educate and empower many with the tools and solutions that work in seeking fairness and financial protection. We are not fighting a minor percentage of mistakes; we are seeking justice from a system that allows rogue human beings, in a position of power, to abuse it! The Enquiries into the Banks should be a criminal enquiry into fraud, manipulation, the monetary gain by deception.

Every deed that has been overturned after the decision had been passed down and executed, allowed the bankers to get away with questionable actions and ultimately devastation to human lives. Regardless of the outcome no Bank will enter into an admission of wrongdoing. That is just how it is! The results depict the extent of the cover up. Finally, after the Head of Management/Legal had been made aware and understood that the actions of the Bankers, used the internal system to camouflage their unconscionable conduct, a fair outcome was derived.

The usual suspects or tag team were prominent in the construction of facilities that would leave the customer vulnerable and dependent. The introducer (Broker) who would usually be referred to by an accountant and in some cases the accountant would refer clients directly to a relationship banker (of choice). These mediated results make it even more important to expose the flaws in not only the business model but also the regulatory organizations monitoring the Banks.

During these procedures the problem is actually getting an opportunity to be able to present your version of events to a decision maker. Instead, on many occasions it would be a stand- off situation with the actual relationship banker and I having had some colourful Brokers get overly defensive and even threatening. Sadly, even with all the complaints made to FOS or ASIC, these people were still protected within the internal systems of Banking.

ASIC is another story; many still continue to manipulate the internal systems of ASIC also leaving a trail of despair. We hear so many 'stories' being more vocal yet not much is done as many lose faith in the organizations policing and protecting us from these very issues. But to be fair ASIC cannot undertake actions when they are hidden between the lines of the documentation that insists everything is done correctly.

So getting to a higher management level such as a Director (who is technically responsible personally for the running of a business, including the actions of his or her staff) or CEO is even harder than seeking an appointment with the prime minister..

Why is that, given their obligations and duties?

Or are these particular CEOs, Directors, and Board members exempt from the standard obligations and laws?

In all these cases they have been people who have tried every avenue of the law, sought out the regularity organisations, made numerous complaints to Ombudsman, and ultimately had nowhere to turn after years of despair and frustration.

You see the professionals already left these guys destitute. Some already had rulings and a few were actually bankrupted by the courts! Many had been to consultants who took what little money they could muster, ultimately to get nowhere. Leaving more devastation and despair, allowing a vulture's fest to begin and hurt even more people. Many knowing that the law is on the Bankers side and that they were not going to make much of a difference.

Yes time is money and we all need to be paid however if you cannot assist then dismiss the opportunity to simple make a quick dollar.

To some degree, this was my cost of a university degree, which I did not plan to study, the wrong doers made it awfully hard to assist anyone. People that had placed trust in other professionals that took their money and left them without time or money and still no result.

I am not a lawyer, even though that was a childhood dream!

I am not an accountant, although I learnt all about accounting and business, I have no degree, never having the opportunity to go to school, much less university. Just because I don't have an MBA, CPA, or any other letters of the alphabet, does not mean I have no qualifications. Perhaps I can place UOL (University of Life) next to my name and it may make a difference as to how people respond!

The results speak volumes as I have gone up against the best Lawyers and most prominent business people. Basically I have always risen to the challenge and found myself seeking justice in a world of corruption.

Over the last 5 years, we have heard nothing but discovery of once reputable people and organisations being exposed for fraud, unscrupulous activities, and deceit ... from Politics and more recently an ATO fraud matter, still under investigation. No doubt there will be more situations that are finally exposed before this book goes to print! Company directors have exploited workers and suppliers for decades, without recourse. They simply create a lifestyle for themselves and then after a certain time and certain debts to the ATO and others, they simply close down and re-establish another business.

ASIC cannot investigate even when there is proof, it sounds easy to make a complaint and ask for a matter to be investigated, however it becomes disheartening when you are told "there is nothing we can do!" Especially when you had lost so much as these people continue to live their extravagant lifestyles while you struggle to deal with the losses caused by their lack of care. We hear of Charities exploiting people's generosity as the government hands out taxpayers' dollars in grants. Millions of dollars are given to organisations that have misappropriated the funds for their own benefits. Do taxpayers pay the bill for the added expenses and losses for yet another enquiry or legal matter?

Temptation is everywhere, but it is those who are in powerful positions that get away with the deceit, as I always say, *"lies have short legs and can't run very far."...MC*

If you are on the receiving end there is only one problem: it's difficult to defend when Bank's have deep pockets and so do many others who have too much to lose if exposed. Really, it's the consumer's funds that the banks use, to defend themselves, so it's a lose/lose situation. Like signing up for a loan, it either 'yes or yes', what choice do you have at the end of the day...Go to a loan shark, in this incestuous river.

In the matters I have investigated, assisted, and scrutinized, not every customer comes with clean hands, (meaning they did not encourage the actions taken by the banker; clean hands also a legal term) these customers desperately wanted money knowing they were not eligible and encouraged the Banker.

One particular situation ended up being a win/win for both parties, but they were actually both in the wrong and they were both better off coming to an amicable resolve. The customer in this instance had the ability to use his family's security, received an approved facility, however due to various issues with another Bank was now facing eviction. We had stopped the eviction and entered into a better agreement that was fair to both sides. I am not a lawyer, just a voice for the customer's that were bankrupted and were not being heard. The customer, represented themselves, I helped them put the pieces together and eliminated the BS.

A Deed of Forbearance with a difference was entered into and has now provided security for both parties. This leads me to the next subject.

2. Desperate People do desperate things!

Yes, unfortunately, this is a fact of L.I.F.E.

There are also many cases where it takes two to Tango (done better on a dance floor than with a Bank!), meaning that some get into problems and start thinking irrationally, looking for a quick fix. This is where all sorts of deceit come into an already-bad situation; whether it is intentional or not, it is wrong.

"If you can't talk about it, you generally shouldn't Do It!" ... MC

When you are faced with losing everything and have a potential resource, it is hard not to act on impulse and take advantage. *Example: A parent entrusts you with a POA (Power of Attorney); they are elderly and have retired in their hometown, also not wanting to burden you any longer. This document allows many things to occur on their behalf (without disclosure or approval!).*

Now, if you are faced with another bank looking at foreclosure, repossession, or worse and you had no available funds, **what would you do?**

This particular person went to the trusted broker to

whom he was referred, "a man that can get any loan approved," as he was known. So, after the initial consultation, it was decided that the broker would "take care of it, he had internal connections!" Really!!

Relief is the only emotion that the customer feels right now, until later when he realises this sounds too good to be true... it was! No one explained the ramifications or the obligations.

Documents are ready to sign and the emotional rollercoaster begins, as you near the office your stomach starts to play a symphony as the knots are twisting and turning. Your broker starts to tell you all is well; **however** ... even with the "friendly" banker, he was unable to get the facility in the customer's name. *The knots tighten in your stomach! Secretly you know it is wrong, but you are desperate!*

He places the documents in front of you strategically marked for signing (execution) as he points out that the only way to do this is in the Father's name ... that's no problem, the broker continues ... you have the POA! (Power of Attorney)

What would you do?

Without trying to come across as a wonderful person that would not do this to their parents, consider what you would do if the opportunity to delay another Bank from taking everything from you and your family? We really cannot judge anyone until you have been in his or her position. Even then some shoes are too uncomfortable to stand in much less walk in. These people are the ones that are usually taken advantage of (set-up) and then exploited by the system, considering that they should never have been approved for such facilities.

But you signed and executed an agreement, now good luck trying to dispute it.

Many and even I would be tempted. You are facing a do-or-die situation with so much pressure because you have one chance to fight and survive and keep a roof over your family's head. You already feel like a failure and do not know how to cope with the emotional cocktail others are initiating you to drink!

"Like eating the forbidden fruit, it will probably taste good for a while but it won't satisfy your appetite. The rotten apple is accepted due to the hunger and that is when you are poisoned".

So, this son has now executed the agreement, has received the funds, and tried to pay for professionals to help him fight off another Bank. (Let's call it B1)

It didn't end so well because this fight was bigger than he could have imagined and dealing with a major bank that had its own agenda (acquiring another bank; one in distress) no one could have been prepared for. As a customer, you are not privy to the real truth, the internal system that allows Bad Apples to abuse their Position of Power. The son and his siblings were declared Bankrupt, initiated by the bank (B1). The other bank, let's call it B2, which had given the facility to the Father (unbeknown to him) were still continuing to speak to the son, regardless of him being bankrupt.

B2 repayments were defaulting due to lack of funds because the entire family now lived on welfare and was constantly asking for help from the father, who was unaware of what was happening to his home and retirement. (A humble home and nothing lavish.) B2 then sent a notice that it could not speak to the son any longer after accepting a large payment for the arrears (borrowed money). Eventually, B2 sent notice of default demand, and ultimately Possession.

In this case both were at fault. I came into this because I was already looking into the B1 matter (undisclosed issues) and at the tail end of things. We stopped the eviction and I had an opportunity to speak to the B2 and its well-appointed lawyers. A Deed of Forbearance was agreed upon and this was the best outcome for all parties. Credit goes to B2 as an organisation because it saw the error. Even though in a court of law the decision would have been an estoppel situation (meaning a signed authority to execute the agreement is almost impossible to overturn as is a previous judgement basically). The agreement is one that shocked another lawyer who was familiar with the entire matter. So, not all banks are unreasonable, even though the bank will still be guaranteed repayment of the loan. It accepted the terms proposed and the family remains in the home and the father will not lose his home.

This particular person still has an ongoing issue with B1, like many others who had been caught between the ongoing sagas of Bankwest being bought out by the Commonwealth Bank of Australia (CBA). Now, that is another can of worms that has infested an Orchard of healthy businesses during the acquisition, only to carry out the expulsion of the crop afterwards. Bankwest had a large commercial lending portfolio and was an aggressive player in the industry, until its parent company instructed that they were not funding the Australian branch and in 2008 the CBA had purchased the Bank ... or should I say, they purchased the loan Book that's what is important to this type of business!

This is a simple explanation, however, rather than

going into the entire details or the allegations as to how and why it easier to comprehend that every bank's value would have to be in its loan book. Bankwest, however, continued actively to seek out customers in a period that would be classified as "trading insolvent," **had it been any other business.**

Example: If a business is told its funding had been stopped by its parent company while it had a sufficient debt without capital, wouldn't it be classified as trading insolvent if it continued to participate in further activities? Not in the case of a Bank that is in the business of manipulating currency, creating multiple amounts compared to the actual deposits or capital held. Banking businesses allows you to run a profitable company that is allowed to take risks because it is guaranteed a Bailout or will it come to a Bail In, like in many places around the world? In Europe, banks took all the deposits made by its customer; this happened in the USA, UK, and it was mentioned in the G20 summit!

Australia follows everyone else, so what's the likelihood? Every business would love to have the same ability? Technically customers or members as we are known to APRA, fund the businesses and we do not have our own union representative to protect us!

Issues still remain too hard or complicated that it is easier just to see the documents as right and the actions leading to them irrelevant.

Having been in the construction industry for decades, I was very familiar with Development projects and the requirements needed by not only the business, but also the banks. Therefore, prior to all of these university assignments (matters), I was paid as a consultant; so I embarked on a journey that saw me consumed with seeking justice and finding a solution. Having been able to derive a living and a talent. in the gentleman's club, (meaning I'd have to prove myself x100!) I was abled to continue on this personal crusade..However now it didn't really matter, this was a world of professionals that didn't listen to you if you didn't work for a Law Firm or had a piece of paper to introduce what education facility declared you capable!

So this is how and why I am now doing this ... giving you the whole ugly truth and hopefully a whole new perspective and ability to protect your Assets (YOU).

The Banks have always run their business in the same manner and they are the ones that should be responsible for the heartache caused by their reckless procedures. Knowing that history is repeating and they keep following the cycle of abuse in complete denial that they are harvesting perpetrators.

So what I've done is break up parts of the publicised Code of Practice; and the issue that I have is that nothing "flows," doesn't make sense, and that could be because the Bank's own documents are so confusing and convoluted. Therefore, as you read it, understand that I have placed various scenarios that contradict the proposed codes.

We all need to be aware of what Banking, Money, and Currency truly means because Banks are a Business with more Power than any other. They can be as reckless as they will be when it comes to the mismanaged lending practices because they have a Bailout and Bail- In option. Do we really believe that our government has a trillion dollars to Bailout the Big Four if we do experience a crisis? I guess the Bail-In option will help!

So here we go, as Diva begins its journey to Banking Beyond Men and creating an equal playing field for the future generations.

The sad reality, which is repetitive in the matters, that I have been involved or have assisted with, is that most of the time the wife or partner had been the last really to comprehend what was going on. Not truly understanding the implications financing a home and running a business entailed and how it related to the funding arrangements, especially when it is mixed in with a business. She supported her partner, signed a document using her emotional DNA. Then she had to face losing her home when the Banks didn't want the risk any longer. They also become more defensive and ignorant to a certain degree. I did it; too, even after all I thought I knew! We all want to be right, our Egos kick in even though you start questioning everything around you and blaming yourself for not seeing the signs? I even questioned my own ability in judging people's characters. **What signs are you expected to spot?** That is when you need to utilise all resources, become responsible, and take control, because it is your name, your future, and the livelihood of all around you at stake.

PART A: INTRODUCTION TO AUSSIE BANKS

3. Introduction to banking but not what others tell you.

Banking began in 1817 (1+8+1+7 = 8 – Is that an auspicious number in numerology or what!). The first bank was called the Bank of New South Wales, established in Sydney. Edward Smith Hall was its cashier and secretary. Not much has changed since this man was in charge, except there is more abuse of power. Now that is something we all know, thanks to Mr. Google!

Soon the branches spread, a plant was seeded, and now it was forming a harvest of Apple trees. This occurred during the 19th & 20th Centuries. So, in 1835, another specimen was planted in Australia by a London-based bank and no doubt another distinguished man. From here the Bank of Australasia then became the ANZ Bank, but only after it merged with many other London-based banks, creating the biggest merger back then. *Wow, how things haven't changed!* *Banks becoming giants in the financial and economic sectors as we get weaker and more dependent on them, that is now becoming more and more evident as the insurmountable enquires and news of questionable conduct continues.*

We found ourselves having various legal tender throughout the States and in 1910 the pound was introduced, so then all states would have to conform to the Bank Notes Tax Act 1910. A tax of 10% per annum on all banks! This was initiated by the Commonwealth. It could have something to do with the Australian Banking Crisis in 1893! Due to the Banks not being regulated, they were **freely lending** with no central bank and no government-provided guarantees.

The Commercial Banks lent heavily and then, in 1888 **(wow, what a number, perhaps numerology wasn't so big those days!),** asset prices collapsed and companies went Bankrupt. It hit crisis point when the Federal Bank failed in 1893, 11 commercial banks around the country stopped trading. *They really had a great business and it would only expand! Except, somehow Risk Management was not a priority and not that much has changed really. Yes, we now are over-regulated in appearance but are the regulations effective? Money is a necessity, after all, so could these wealthy and intelligent men not foresee the inevitable? Surely what goes up must eventually come down, as the same events have continued throughout the years, even now in the21st century.*

In 1911, a new crop of apples was planted, called the Commonwealth Bank, established by the Federal government; and, by 1913 was in six states. During the Great Depression, it took over many failed banks, including 2 state savings banks; the Government Savings Bank of NSW and the State Savings Bank of WA. In 1991, it took over the State Bank if Victoria. These guys were unstoppable! This harvest was sure to produce many apples, let's hope they were not **rotten** or infested with a disease called **greed** or they may contaminate the **system, worse**!

Now that's the basic history on Banks, but somehow after all the time I've spent defending the voiceless – and I isn't a lawyer – mediating at various forums, I don't see much change. Perhaps I need stronger lens in my reading glasses because I still don't see it. Claims that we have had so many reviews of reforms, reporting to regulators, improvement to Codes or regulations, however all based on the initial principal, so what internal reforms have made a difference? Currently there have been tighter restrictions and regulators created to monitor reporting, compliance, and complaints. Yet the news exposed more issues to contradict these new or old regulations. They can always be manipulated by a Bad Apple.

If you look deeper into history, the banks were divided into a savings bank (run by the State) that paid practically no interest (for using peoples' money) and they were restricted to providing mortgages (fast forward to 2015 and they'd be laughing now!). Merchant Banks were a Trading Bank and didn't offer services to the general public. So, that made room for little banks to plant a crop that was not regulated as heavily. They produced a number of rotten apples, without as much notice to the general eye.

The Commonwealth Bank also did central bank functions and it was in 1920, during World War II, that other banks were getting the shits and feeling discomfort, so the Reserve Bank was established on the 14th January 1960. So, they held the lead up until then I guess. CBA is a powerful Giant, even back then! (Basic Language used, we don't need the vocabulary of professionals that confuse the situation)

After this, the banks were gradually released to operate as a merchant bank now able to set their own interest rates. I am gathering CBA was the largest player, given it was government owned. A Bank of the People … not certain who took priority, however. Many would say that back then the Bank was for the people but that all started to change and now it's about more people for the Banks.

———

These guys had it made; hopefully, they took care of their wives, too! New technology was adopted and in 1969 (great year) automated teller machines (ATM) were introduced. A new type of harvest was developed and now it's been used to launder money, could this wall-mounted washing machine continue to spin benefit to the Banks? In 1983 the Aussie dollar was floated. Now we were playing with the Big Boys.

The 1980s were yet another unstable time for the banks, some surviving and other being swallowed up by the larger banks (the Big Four). For whatever reason, the government relinquished its direct ownership of the banks and CBA was fully privatised by 1996.Now others owned the Banks; who knew what would, could and ultimately did happen.

More Non-Banking lenders provided securitised home loans and in 1998 any omission/misunderstanding of the banks was transferred from the RBA to the Australian Prudential Regulation Authority (APRA), which is funded by the Banks. Does that protect the customer when the institution with which you are disputing, funds the organisation that is regulating and keeping these businesses honest?

Who keeps who employed? Whose ethics would

you protect if your future were at stake? I am not certain if that was always the case, but it certainly is now, the Banks feed all our regulatory watchdogs. So how vicious would that dog actually be against his master? I wouldn't count on it as being a great guard dog for our protection, and more like a loyal pup to its master!

Anyhow, I digress, history is important and that is why it is taught at school. The only problem is that we have carried this history into our future with minimal change. Before some of you start to critique my comments, just look back each time there was a boom in the housing market and then the crash. How is a bank allowed to go all out and lend freely, knowing the house price is exaggerated. It reaches an astronomical amount of lending on their books and only now tightens its lending practices, when we are in a trillion dollar debt? First, they place you in a debt knowing you will not be able to sustain it when anything changes. It is certain, too. What are we not following here? Some school kids get it and others still don't know what a Bad rating is all about!

Who is in the best position to monitor and foresee what potentially happens regarding the economy and according to history?

I will elaborate with real scenarios throughout the

book.

So, back to the rules and regulations, (another explanation for terms and conditions) these are now governed by APRA and there was a Payment System Board, too. In 1996, the Aussie Government established the Financial System Inquiry. This was due to the many stuff ups in regard to the deregulation period. Perhaps this is where the loopholes were discovered. Today, we are still seeking answers as to why and how so many customers have actually been failed by the Banking System and rarely will the Bank admit that there was any wrong doing on its part, just follow the paper trail ... that will prove it! Could that be because in Australia we are very litigious?

After this first Inquiry that was chaired by Stan Wallis (the Wallis report), he determined that we needed to have 2 regulators. (So he is the culprit, I wonder if he was a banker in his early days). Now we have Australian Securities and Investment Commission (ASIC) and APRA? We come to the establishment of another regulator or three because we then have the Financial Services Ombudsman (FOS) and Credit and Investment Ombudsman (CIO). Here is where we all need to really "get it," because of the many codes of conduct, practice, regulations, and everything else.

It can be very contradicting … in order to understand one you need to know if another counteracts it! Never will I say I'm *"unedumacated"* after reading them so many times over. The problem was that the more I read up on the regulations and obligations, the more confused and frustrated I got. How the hell is anyone to understand this when it appears to be conflicting with what actually happens? The actions of a Bad Apple are concealed by the jargon within the various codes; these make it easier to cover the trails of manipulation and denial. As it appears that the system is actually regulated.

My point to this is that a person is behind the actions that take place (pre and post any facility or transaction) are not monitored and what they say opposed to what they actually do often differs. It is all well and good to impose a bunch of rules and regulations and assume they will all act accordingly, but how can you be sure. Each specific department or area has its own procedures, yet they all work together to achieve the same result. That is the business model and it can and has been manipulated to conceal the actions of some people who take advantage and abuse the trust bestowed upon them.

In order to understand with what business you are dealing, you would need then to undo the tangled web of company structures and roles they play.

Some Banks (like Credit Unions- the only difference is the criteria for its memberships really, it claims to be a Not For Profit because customers are ultimately the members?) are still not as regulated, then we have all the subsidiary banks whose parent company is usually one of the Big 4.Macquarie Bank is another beast in itself and has various arms of financial planning and offers all the bells and whistles, but has varying regulations but ultimately it runs the same businesses.

Again the same issue relates to this ... it's human nature with which we are dealing with as well as the system that allows them to act on their temptations leading to abuse.

The Banks all vary and, although they are categorised by the license, they all hold and have obligations to various regulators; they are all the same. They all follow the same procedures and codes of conduct (plus all the other legislation); however, they are all able to abuse you financially. Emotional and physical abuse has resulted when things go wrong.

They take your money; they lend you money while they ensure they take all your assets for security. The whole process starts with a banker (person) who does have an agenda, they want your business, they want to you to sign up to a facility. Good, Bad, or Indifferent, that is their job after all. They befriend you as they break down your walls of resistance, and you confide in them. This stranger has instantly gained your trust as he says all the right words and performs all the right moves, using the emotional triggers you have innocently exposed. Your natural defenses are now disarmed.

It's like you are an older style of smoke detector (not hardwired like the newer version) and the banker has managed to remove the battery so there is no way your natural beeper will go off, when the signs show of any danger. Instead, as the smoke thickens and flames start to appear, your banker eases your concerns as he disarms your emotional reaction to certain changes you noticed. It's too late when the damage is done and you are left gasping for air. The only option you have is to attempt to walk through the flames.

"Why didn't you do something, the Fire-fighter questions?" (Management) You did and you were obedient and followed every obligation, you relied on this person. You could not see the truth behind the grin of the smiling assassin as he now gets away with attempted murder and the judges blame you!

This stranger that has befriended you can destroy you because they decide your future, then suddenly the Bank has no appetite for your business any longer ... directed by the employee of the bank, your friend and confidant the banker! How hard is that to understand? Your asset is no longer valuable enough to remain and needs to move on...but to who and How? Is there another reason behind your default?

You have to protect yourself and be confident dealing with a Business that holds an advantage over everyone, including our government.

"*Money is a tool and we all need it to survive, to be healthy, and to provide for the future; but it is a business for the banks. Don't allow your emotions to control your decisions when dealing with Goliath. The thing is that you are dealing with another human being whose role is to sign you up to make a profit for his or her employer. That is the truth and this person is not your friend or partner, no matter how accommodating he/she is!*" *(Reality Check)*

By the way, so that I don't sound too one-sided, we have evolved considering more women are now employed as tellers/bankers. But, realistically it began as a Man's domain; just saying! Dealing with the Bad Apples there is still a larger number of males who will use the system to feed their egos, wallets, and positions. There is good, bad, and, as I say, indifferent in all of us; but to become a Bad

Apple, you had to have a rotten seed planted for it to grow.

Women have entered corporate positions in Banks that were mainly male dominated, and I have met a few who are all exceptional people. They are leaders, having the highest of integrity and instinct to do good for all females because they are also Role models.

The fear around this is that it takes an even stronger-willed woman to stand for change and not be pulled into the same cycle. It is tough in a Male-dominated industry not to conform and lose your femininity; a Lonely Journey at times and a costly investment for Change. Some have been placed in a Powerful role to be used as a scapegoat, someone else to blame for a system initiated by men, and who better than a woman. Certain events occur to introduce a false sense of equality, especially when all avenues of diversion have failed; a target is needed in order to distract from what really needs to be done.

We are emotional beings no matter how strong and staunch you may appear. There are those who believe that they are clever and have it all worked out; watch out because many have agreed to things because of their ego. Ultimately, emotions play a role when signing up for almost anything.

Even the multimillionaires get excited at the next deal. There is always an emotion involved, the excitement, eagerness, determination, and at times desperation in obtaining funding to get ahead: A home you want to purchase, an investment or a development, a business you want to get off the ground, all valid reasons. All are exciting and all are emotions that can be easily persuaded by a well-versed salesman! Sadly, the most damaging emotion is the panic and despair when things get too difficult to manage.

The truth is that as we continue to fight the well-written agreements that have been thoroughly executed in exchange for money. They are mainly constructed for the bank's protection regardless of the Double Dutch clauses perceived to be for your protection. So, no matter what the story of events really is, it is the document that counts at all times, no matter what. Subsequently we continue to go to the extreme and challenge these documents after the fact (when it revealed you are no longer worthy). The truth is that what you thought you were signing weren't the words that sounded when your friendly banker was explaining them. So you sign; this is now and considered "bad luck, you signed it," (Hypothetically) regardless of the legal explanation and examples, they all come back to this! 'You can undo what you've signed…it's admitting you agree to whatever you don't really understand'

All the Codes of Whatever, you have acknowledged that you understood AND you actually read them … did you? Many don't bother until it is too late and some have never even sighted them until it was pointed out!

The Banking system stems back for centuries now and it truly hasn't fundamentally changed, it's just been reworded and has more regulators that appear to be on your side. Unfortunately, they, too, have been tailored to conceal what they cannot undo, especially when the jurisdictions are conveniently placed to exclude many complainants.

It's not the Bank that is the problem; it's the people in power who benefit from the internal systems. We were all taught not to talk to strangers and be wary, always protect yourself (your asset).However this stranger that you have entrusted with your financial future, and your LIFE, you gift him instantly with your TRUST. We somehow forget about stranger danger. Why, because you're in a vulnerable position and this person is your friend… right … wrong!

   * This person usually neglects to tell you what you don't want to hear but should know.

* This person doesn't show you the notes he put on your file.

* This person says he is transparent, but continues to set you up for his own gain (how would you know?).

* This person has no reason to help you when he has been helping himself.

- It all depends on the nature of the Bad Apple ___Not all bankers are Bad Apples, let us be clear on this – there is good and bad in everyone and not all of us use our positions to Abuse another human being!___

For this purpose, we are only speaking (writing) of the Bad Apples just to clarify the percentage quoted by senior management of a Bank at 1% - it's more, but even when I humoured him, it's 1% too many given the extent of our indebtedness to banks!

What you do not realise is that they are furnished with the right documentation and procedures so that they are in control of your Life, I meant FILE. (Practically the same!) Your problems begin here ... they have Goliath on their side, with every support system available. Including the regulators who are now disempowered because they cannot overturn a judicial decision and a signed document. ***Don't sign a Deed of Forbearance too quickly.*** If an employee of a bank is corrupted by the temptations availed to him, then you are destined to end up with food poisoning or worse. The undisclosed agenda between employees of these businesses allow them the rights to use, manipulate, and prearrange your demise. All the while appearing to have performed his duties by the book, the codes that they endeavour to implement.

That is the real problem.

If there is only 1% of Bad Apples in each bank, then that is enough to infest the entire harvest. Currently I'd say there are 25% and counting, with no real pesticides.

These tales are of real experiences very true and the emotions are raw, but there are stories also of triumph against a Goliath that is a protected species and continues to cause destruction.

So, keep reading if you are slightly interested in knowing what you think you know only to discover that there is always something you don't!

The problem we face is that we really do not pay attention to the pamphlets and fine print we are NOT clearly instructed to read and understand the **Code** of Practice and or terms and conditions ... not to mention every other Code or regulation that you discover is relied upon when you are deep *shit* or on the verge of hardship. Really? How does a bank with the multitude of departments and employees of today mange to police each individual person, ensuring he is not acting inappropriately? They do deserve the salaries they pay themselves, if they manage all this and can claim that we will never discover an intentional human error amongst their staff. But, seriously, how do they manage it? Human nature is difficult to manage at the best of times and many employees have all come from another Bank. The fear is that the new crop will be infested by the percentage of bad apples. I cannot see how these Codes of Conduct/Practises or any other Code can enforce the obligations of a person who is power driven by greed and ego to do the ethical thing much less the right thing!

Then I read that these are a "guideline" only? There is no recourse for a human who can potential destroy a family's financial future if he doesn't follow **good** practices and who defines what that **good** practice necessitates?

Basically it states, "we endeavour to, but if we don't then don't blame us as employers." That is my interpretation because I was told to refer to this Code of Practice a few times when various employers denied any wrong doing by their employees! ... Having been told that an employee was able to override the system to change dates and issue notices at their discretion. Yet, no one saw this as a problem? Even when shown the evidence the employer managed to deny the action ever taking place!

Life has a way of depicting the terms given by professional as a load of

POOP (Professional Opportunistic Oversights Permissible) – *My view only not a real term*

With all the evidenced examples of Financial Abuse caused by an employee of a Bank, we continue to protect internal manipulation of an organisation that ultimately holds the keys to the country. If we are to be realistic and review the answers provided by the CEOs' (Chief Executive Officers) to the many question put to them during the enquiries, they all refer to the economy. Is this a threat? … Especially when they are contributors to the overall problem, whilst they show multi-million-dollar profits. (Here comes another can of worms to infest the crop and not benefit the soil)

Whilst completing and reviewing the series of books about banks, a news story breaks out: CBA is at the centre of AUSTRAC court proceedings. Just another in a string of recent discoveries of questionable conduct, this goes beyond the manipulation of individual files. The bank accepted deposits totaling millions and millions of dollars through its ingenious ATMs or, more specifically, IDM (deposits through an ATM) without reporting the transactions quickly and efficiently.

So let's refer to the Codes of Practice-Conduct-Credit-Privacy and any other regulating legislation until we get to the different types of Law of obvious. But, then, if you did all of this you would surely miss the opportunity to get the funding you need because it's already taken weeks to get to an offer and now your time is cut short. So, you forget about what could go wrong and usually convince yourself that it won't. Until it does and then you are referred to what you thought was marketing junk mail. This allowed the Business all rights to change their risk appetite and breech in areas you never thought possible.

3.1　The Code is there for the Bank to follow, but what happens when it's not? That is when we are legislated by the other governing bodies, except you need to meet their jurisdictions. In other words, you should read and understand their policies and procedures also. Regardless, this Code would have us believe that because it is written it is obeyed, especially with other regulatory bodies. We are protected! Right?

WRONG

This is only a standard. There is nothing that has been evidenced that these codes must be practiced. Once you sign an agreement you have signed your rights away.

In the workshop, we have broken down all banking documents to show you in simple terms what you are signing. No matter how great your lawyer is, not all is disclosed and it is a legal and costly battle you will almost always face. Regardless of your situation, there are things you won't know ... no matter how smart you are. There is only so much a anyone else will do for you. So you need the tools to be able to take control and responsibility for your life.

4. Code Explained

These are my Codes for the Book:

Bank – A Business that is a for-profit entity also;

Apples – bankers

Banker – employee of an employer (Bank)

Orchard – A plantation from which a particular harvest is generated. (Banking system)

Bad Apples – Rogue employee

All definitions on the last few pages is what you will find in the Code of Practice, which is a public document for all to read and comprehend as they will, including the Banks.

All Bank-related documents have been transcribed into understandable terminology in other e-books produced by Diva Enterprises so that you can understand for what you are actually signing up. They are based on actual results throughout many mediated cases, with favourable results.

Please note, when I first dealt with the Banks I was a simpleton to them and I viewed myself as such, until I had to fight for my own Asset, the one that housed my three children. I have since gone on to resolve many matters and all these families were voiceless warriors that continued to search for the answers concealed by many professionals and the system.

PART B: ARE THEY REALLY COMMITTED TO YOU

5.   The Code states that a Bank is committed to you.

The Bank should consider it needs your money actually to have a business! A business committed to making more profits, So why wouldn't it make such a statement? Without you it has no business! A bank is reliant on you as a customer to deposit money so it can in turn create profit from it. Imagine if we all withdrew our money, at the same time, one bank at a time. Then whilst it has enforced a debt culture, we are obligated to it, and it can also punish you for it … so, buyer beware! *You are the customer, much the same as a retail shopper, so you have a variety of options; however, the principals are very much the same. The difference is you cannot get a refund.*

6. The Banks claim that they will:

(a) **Promote better-informed decisions about our banking services:** Does this mean they will finally be transparent? It wasn't until numerous enquires that the public is now able to request a copy of bank valuations on its assets (that they paid for), or at least sight them! How transparent is it being when you have no idea what notes are made on your file and your internal information?

Tolerate with this and I'll give you an example!

(i) By providing effective disclosure of information: This is definitely not the case and if it is, can someone show me where this is done and in "which Bank?"

(ii) By explaining to **you**, when asked, the contents of brochures and other written information about **banking services**: Please tell me how many times do you stop to think "I should really ask to about all the pretty looking pamphlets and booklets that look like 'junk mail,'" and on the odd occasion that you do receive these, how many times have you treated it as it appears … junk mail or promotional material?

Shouldn't the Employee (part of the produce) make it a point to tell you that "should anything go wrong with your facility, we can rely on these booklets to recall our money!" The words that form part of the acceptance that you signed when going for a facility as you sit at a desk all excited that you weren't rejected. We've all been there! … Unless you are cash rich and don't need credit. Finance is a necessity, yet it's also a privilege to a degree and it's pretty special when you are approved and made to feel worthy of the Bank's acceptance into its business.

So, this booklet or pamphlet of terms and condition in fine print, after promoting credit facilities, is generally overlooked at the best of times.

I certainly didn't and I trusted not only my banker (a bad apple, I discovered much later!), but I trusted my accountant (who also introduced a lot of business to this particular Bad Apple)

Here I always thought it was promoting more Banking services and nothing more.

If you* ask *us for advice on banking services:

Does this mean that every banker (employee) is authorised? A relationship banker was always my point of call and they actually told me that my best option was to keep one of my facilities separate. He also signed me up to facilities he assured me was best.

How do customers tell who is and isn't authorised when all employees are ever so willing to sign you up to another facility, especially to keep you within their business.

Q: Does this also mean that every banker should be licensed also given that they do give advice on the best possible product for your needs?

A. *By referring **you** to appropriate external sources of advice;*

Is this when a banker refers you to a broker with whom he has a working relationship or is it the case like some banks that have undisclosed affiliation to a brokerage business?

Who protects you from advice given between a broker and a banker, especially when the same employer affiliates them all?

B. *By recommending that **you** seek advice from someone such as **Your** legal or financial adviser;*

This statement relates to the one above doesn't it? But then again if it is written a number of times, the Banks is protected and you are confused because you did not seek legal advice. You would have gone to a Broker (like many of us have) or you are so trusting that you WAIVE this right upon signing the documents. In many cases you simply trust and sign.

Then there is the other scenario; you know the one where you have now waited for an approval and the time bomb is ticking! Then the trust is even more important and duty of care (to yourself) is non-existent. The Banker/Broker will *finally* provide the funding you have now become desperate to complete and have drawn down. Regardless that the facility terms are something different to what you believed it was (as explained by Broker & Banker)! I can clearly recall my relationship manager (who owned the Bank, or was a franchisee?) walked me across the road from the bank and I signed in front of another professional. I didn't realize this was a regular thing for the pair!

This was POOP! **Practices** **Organised** by **O**verpowering **PROFESSIONALS**

Minor decisions are made with your head but nearly all-Major decisions are made from the Heart...Diva L.I.F.E Tip

Previously and even to date there are documents being signed without them being taken to a lawyer to explain, even then are they truthfully explained? Many of them are so one sided and border on being deemed unfair, so why aren't they disputed or amended by your legal representative before you sign them?

Does this mean that if a lawyer disagreed with the documents they could be amended *(not that many lawyers dispute them, lawyers are used as witnesses more times than not!)* and would the LAW allow it?

Doesn't the Lawyer understand that it is **harder** to defend once it has been signed...I think it falls under **estoppel**, but I am no lawyer!! If this were to happen many people would be without a job and banking would have Made to Measure Mortgage documents (Banking Beyond Men®)

Would the Laws have to be rewritten to accommodate such a thing? It happens with other matters involving contracts, so why do Banks not have to conform?

Banking Beyond Men have created the Made to Measure Mortgage Banking Model to avoid the emotional pain that is attached to funding.

Throughout every matter that had to be reopened it was clear that the emotional and humane component was not considered. The documents show no feels but the decision were emotion induced. So we do use heart to make the biggest decision that impacts our financial future. We only think we use our Heads.

Guys must remember that EGO is an emotion; male-to-male you all want to appear intelligent. (No offence intended)

(b) *Provide general information about the rights and obligations that arise out of the banker and customer relationship in relation to banking services;*

This one is a real confusion bomb! It is very contradictory because every person I know befriended his or her bank manager/

relationship manager. I have given you a few scenarios of these situations throughout the book.

Employees of Banks can come across as your new BFF and some act like your business partner. The problem is they can become your worst enemy when they move your file for the next department to do the dirty work.

Each time I have clearly displayed that the actions of an employee (banker) went above and beyond by misleading the customer; this Code is mentioned along with others. That a Bank is not your business partner (summarized) and a banker shall not involve himself in the daily running of your business.

BUYER BEWARE: there are a number of excuses as to what is classified as daily running of your affairs. So, when we advise the relationship bank manager (RBM) of actions we are taking in our business and he suggests otherwise and tells you its best for your file ... Don't! Do it your way and take responsibility, because he won't! In Fact: It is not a defense no matter how clearly it shows; ultimately the Banker will be cautious not to have this documented so do not count on the spoken word alone...Always insist on the written word! Just like they do!!

(c)   *The Code states that the Bank will Provide information to you in plain language;*

This should probably read: **our employees will provide information verbally to make it sound easy for you to sign the documents willingly, even when you do not understand or agree with the contents.**

So, BEWARE – the documents are binding and you need a degree to comprehend your obligations and what we can do to your financial wellbeing!

Scenario: In my own situation I had an investment property in the inner city of Sydney and when I went for refinancing the Banker had explained that this investment was a "Stand Alone Facility" (which is what I requested). It would not be collateralised. (Words of the Banker/Manager) Basically, this property was income producing and positively geared. (My retirement and in a Trust) There was no risk for the Bank; this one was a NO BRAINER!

This situation occurred after I actually took on one of the Big Four when I was defending my Home and Investment during the GFC (Global Financial Crisis that I defined as Grab Financial Capital excuse). After an 18-month battle, an agreement was reached and I saved my Assets; God knows they were hard to acquire given my situation, so I learnt all I had to know for that battle! However, my circumstances changed and I was no longer a single mother of 3. I met someone who at the time was demanding within himself, but I felt obligation and wanted the fairy tale I never had. So, when he wanted to move to the sunny Gold Coast, I agreed. (You need to understand the boring details to "get it," so hang in there!) We found a house that was amazing and I doubted we'd be able to buy it, especially when it was my assets and my ability alone, to enable funding! No contribution from the fairy-tale Prince Charming (PC).

Now, regardless, I was refinancing and this particular banker was confident in refinancing my current assets. Loan Value Ratio (LVR) was less than 30% for the investment property and 55% on the value of the Home. Easy ... Right ... Then with a conversation had among PC, the friendly Banker (who came to the house) and myself, the Banker convinced me that this dream home (one that I could not live in for more than 3 months a year due to commitment in Sydney) could be included quite easily. He had an application ready to sign! The excitement from the other parties and I took was shocked but WOW! Except then the pressure I was placed under dulled the excitement as I was the sole provider and my earning capacity was about to change given that I was in this relationship and pleasing another person.

Everything that was told to me by the Banker was not what I signed up for, and I actually believed him when he said, "In 12 months we I will renew the facilities and have them amended to interest only!" I never should have received the facility for the home in the Gold Coast and no matter that I frequently wrote and advised the banker of my concerns and difficulty (as I predicted). He said a number of things but the documents said another.

Even the stand-alone facility, on my particular document, it stated that it was independent of the other facilities so if it was to be sold the Bank had no right to the excess ... That's another story!

This is my own experience and then what followed gives more evidence that this Code is as worthless as the formation of a Word document. Sent to an enemy that is able to amend the contents, save as a PDF, and claim it is an agreement! (You don't trust an enemy, do you?)

These words cannot make a banker, who is God during a time of seeking funds (Money) to create a fairy tale and during these times a mixture of emotions is involved. In my case, there was a lot of pressure, also, but ultimately it's my responsibility no matter the surroundings.

What no one explains to you is that you can defend yourself regardless, even when it seems impossible.

(d) The Code states the Bank will: Monitor external developments relating to banking codes of practice, legislative changes, and related issues. With the lack of transparency and the inability to understand your rights due to a highly legislated industry, how do you determine if this is really the case?

In my situation and that of those I have represented in a mediated forum, this is definitely not adhered to or monitored correctly. Even when the employee (banker) was aware of the change, you are convinced of their dedication to "helping" you (keeping you). The Banker creates a dependency.

Scenario; a number of people were affected when there is a change in banking legislation, be it internal or external, which falls in the category of related issues. This caused major devastation to many families during the GFC – they weren't warned in a time frame, allowing the banks to exercise their rights ... the ones you are usually influenced to ignore and treat as a generic document.

Given that there have been many incorrect (cannot use the word wrong because the codes and documents will dispute that any wrong doing has occurred) practices experienced by too many customers it seems inappropriate to make the statements printed in the Code of Practices. *We will act fairly and reasonably toward **you** in a consistent and ethical manner. In doing so, **we** will consider **your** conduct, **our** conduct, and the contract between us.*

This is difficult to swallow; it's like being

forced to eat a handful of dry crackers and not really certain if your hunger is for a dry biscuit or a nutritious meal. It's all great *having the offering by a stranger that is friendly and ever willing to* ease your uncertain hunger, but then forgetting to give you the dip or a glass of water to wash it down. As you swallow, you have no choice now but to keep going, hoping that all the mechanisms are in place to create saliva to moisten the now-broken-up biscuit. You seek assistance in fear of choking because it blocks your airways and scrapes the lining of your Esophagus while you hold onto hope that this deceiving object reaches your stomach without too much damage!

You will get to read more real scenarios where many have exhausted every avenue, when it comes to regulating authorities and justice, only to be stripped of any remaining funds, credibility, and ultimately left voiceless. The real hurt is that they had to continue living with the ugly truth that all they did wrong was trust a professional – a stranger in a position of power who was protected by the internal mechanisms of the system.

6.2. *The Code will also state that in meeting **its** key commitments to **you, the bank** will follow* *prudential obligations.* How many people actually understand what that means and how many people have ever questioned this during an application for finance?

The Act stems back to 1956 and has been amended, however the fundamentals remain, so how have the regulators adopted the current environment or are we still in the olden days? Back then banks were supposed to be a bank of the people, this would make sense given that without customers there would be no business. Nowadays, Banks have forgotten about the people that have created their businesses and focus on management salaries, shareholders profits, and generating a Debt mentality so that we need them and the Government can't control them. So is that prudential Lending for Banks' purposes?

Q: What is prudential lending? A: Care and Forethought in business. Making certain that the facility will not ruin your financial life. Not placing you in potential hardship!

Q: Can I challenge it? A: Once your Facility is signed up, you can spend a lot of money to challenge it, but ultimately it is difficult to fight within the judicial system. There action you can take yourself to seek fairness. Just make sure you have 'clean hands'

It's like signing a Prenuptial to show your loyalty, love, and dedication and then fighting for your fair share after learning of the lies and deceit

We must remember these are guidelines for the Banks, which has been displayed by the various enquiries and so-called investigations. The simple truth is that although the employee has not obeyed these guidelines and has performed actives that have placed you in a hardship position, or at a loss, they will almost always be acting within the guidelines of the Legal documentation internally. Therefore, when this statement has been raised, it is ignored due to the Legal meanings behind the clauses in your executed documents.

Prudent lending is forgiven after you sign a document counteracting the guidelines and legalising the manipulation of the implied word and actions.

Can you change the document, before signing?

Many of us (girls in particular) learn about finance and money in general by their parents.

Not everyone is academically trained. A lawyer should be able to make the amendments but a Bank does not have to accept. Whilst this is true for all businesses, the Bank has an advantage because it preys on your emotional and financial needs and vulnerabilities. During the credit approval process, while timing also plays a significant part of the lending practice (tactics).

We have broken up the prudential lending requirements and compiled a checklist to give to your bank prior to applying for finance. (Diva workshops targeting school age to adults)

The major issue we face is being able to detect when a professional is abusing his position and how you can protect yourself. What you need to record, what you need to ask and the need to always reiterate conversations in writing.

Management will always deny any unethical behaviour that can be misunderstood by the documentation and the fact that it will always come back to you accepting and acting upon the loan.

We show you the what and what not to do.

7. Compliance with laws

7.1   The Banks will tell us that they adhere to the relevant laws relating to banking services, these were to include everything relating to finance, credit, and deposit taking, plus all other banking services. It would include privacy, discrimination, and all relevant laws; you'd image this to be correct. Sadly there are matters where you may find yourself frustrated and disheartened with the Laws in our country. Issues such as:

(a)   Employees who use your information to benefit their new positions in another institution where they are eager to generate "new" business. *You may not see this as an issue until you find yourself following a trusted banker who has led you into a false sense of security.*

This is not a breach of Privacy apparently, as an employee this person will do things within limitations imposed by standard employment agreements. *Making it ok, even when he passes on information to another fellow banker and the actions are clear to others yet protected by systematic documentation designed to protect the employer.*

An employee knows that after 12 months he can no longer be prosecuted or investigated apparently. This was discovered at a meeting with Head of Legal for a large bank.

(b) How do we define discrimination, when there are many varying definitions and acts in this regard to these laws?

*There are many case studies where the customer was discriminated against and ignored because they were a guarantor and had no say regarding the delinquent account., Facilities that should not have been given in the first place (**prudential lending**)*

A husband who decided to jump ship by informing his wife of 15 years, so she was faced with the cyclone of destruction and had such a hard time trying to pay out the default in order to save her own credit rating. Then the family home was in jeopardy; we worked through this but the injustice remains. The husband has a new home loan with his new partner now, and the same banker at another bank.

This doesn't fall under the terms of discrimination, even though she was never privy to the discussions, correspondence, and agreements. She signed like many of us not wanting to, but emotionally obligated to! However, if we break it down, she was prejudiced; there was unfair treatment and she was denied an opportunity (to clear her name), unequal treatment to that of her husband (she was added as a guarantor only not named on the loan).

Another matter that has recently been resolves saw an elderly man named on a facility he never knew he had, the man is an elderly migrant who lives overseas and had a facility in Sydney on his unencumbered property. It gets worse, as I discovered the Bank had never even spoken to the customer. This humble man wanted to return to his home but became ill and was about to lose his home. Is that discrimination, when he didn't speak a word of English?

There are many circumstances that build up to these positions, but sadly no one pays attention to the action and only the end result. Documentation giving all rights to an Employer who has allowed employees the opportunity to pick and chose their prey.

7.2 When I read this in the Code*: "If this **Code** imposes an obligation on **us**, in addition to obligations applying under a relevant law, **we** will also comply with this **Code** except where doing so would lead to a breach of a law (for example, a privacy law),"*my emotions flare up and I cannot help but feel angered at the contradiction. And I'm an advocate against Abuse!

Many employees of the bank have breached not only their obligations but also the law. We are all focusing on the Banks, but we are neglecting the fact that we are unraveling action carried out by humans (employees), all committed without recourse because Goliath employs them. If this were an ordinary business, the Employer would be liable.

How many businesses are able to cause so much destruction and take so many risks with other peoples' lives and money and then have not only a taxation benefit but a guarantee by the Government ... isn't that taxpayers money anyway?

Not only does it have all these added benefits, but it has a monopoly over most of us and a power that has an ability to engage others to their defense even when the law has clearly been manipulated to suit Goliath.

Not breaching the Law, however, allowing employees to seize the opportunity to gain power and monetary gain. Depending on how rotten the BAD APPLE is, it can form an alliance with a Broker or another person in a powerful position (accountants/lawyers) the professional we entrust with our lives. This creates a web that is even harder to escape, as they all protect each other.

SCENARIO: A Director of a Construction company that had used and kept all his facilities with a particular bank for many years, moved due to the influence of an introducer (Broker)., He is persuaded to change banks while this banker had promised him a better deal; and, what's more comforting when a banker acts and states he is your mate!

"(MANIPULATING ASSURANCE TACTICAL ENTICMENT) BECAREFUL NO MATTER HOW MUCH YOU THINK YOU KNOW THEM...MONEY CHANGES PEOPLE AND IF THEY ARE EVER TO BE PLACED UNDER PRESSURE TO EXPLAIN TO MANAGEMENT, YOU WILL BE THROWN UNDER THE BUS. DO YOU REALLY

THINK THEY'LL LOSE THEIR JOBS OVER YOU?

This is about an ambitious young family man who has a project envied by others and is considered "green" to the industry. Great, right? ... The story is very disturbing because this man was manipulated and sadly by a practice that goes back in time and is still camouflaged.

The banker (employee) decides he has a better opportunity elsewhere, given that during this said period there were a lot of things going on behind the scenes in the Banking Industry. Internally, it was not hard to discover trade secrets, as we call them. So he now leaves and becomes a Broker, watch out that is like a fox in sheep's clothing... BUYERS BEWARE! You now have another caliber of broker, one that knows the system internally and understands what boundaries exist and how to manipulate them. This BAD APPLE is poisonous. He then partners with another BAD APPLE and the rest is history.

But this is not an issue for the employer whatsoever, even though both these employees worked together? You'd think that someone would have looked into this even from a conflict perspective.

The issue with conflict is that is can be covered up as can insider trading within these industries. These particular Bad Apples had gained a considerable property portfolio due to this ability.

Is it me or am I too sensitive to corruption and manipulation or is it just unjust actions of a person in a position of power? After the lessons and my formal and informal education when it comes to surviving abusers, I have a problem with people who abuse the trust innocent people gift them. They disarm the person and use their position to benefit themselves.

First, placing the customer on the emotional rollercoaster and at the same time implying that they will be there to guide them and protect them along the way.

The promise of a Banker.

Back to the story; There were many Codes of Conduct, Conflict, Procedures and Practices that were not adhered to by the Banker and it's employer so that clause should be reworded.

8. Retention of your rights

What rights do you have when you are voiceless?

In addition to **your** rights under this **Code**, **you** retain any rights **you** may have under Federal laws, especially the Trade Practices Act 1974, the Australian Securities and Investments Commission Act 2001, Chapter 7 of the Corporations Act 2001, and under State and Territory laws, especially the Uniform Consumer Credit Code and Fair Trading Acts.

Now this statement started to get even more confusing because the Law is so broad and, having always wanted to be a Lawyer (Family Law), I found myself reading and studying the many books given and bought so I could understand how this was allowed. How are you expected to know all these laws and regulations when, by this stage your funding has been depleted or frozen? You are usually already violated and left bewildered as you try and uncover 'how' this was at al possible?

How can you hold any retention of your rights? It's a bit late after the fact!

Scenario: A facility was provided to a couple that had purchase a new home, whilst they had a friendly banker to whom they spoke openly and when Sharon was retrenched they experienced difficulties. Without going into the entire story, the bank decided that it no longer wanted their facility; it was a risk and was moved from the friendly banker to Collections. The friendly banker turned into an employee of the bank because he conveniently forgot to advise the couple of what was really happening to its file. The couple received a default and demand in the same day. WTF! Panic, fear, and adrenaline has now overtaken the couple as they take out their frustration and distress on each other.

We requested their file and all it contained, it was not provided. You will never see the true internal notes and recordings on your file. You have no rights there. A Broker out of the blue, who knew all about their position, contacted the couple. No one else could have or would have access to their personal details and this is not something you'd post of Facebook!

Then Craig is convinced by the bank's employee (collections team) to sign a Deed of Forbearance immediately to avoid further action. He then pressures Sharon to do the same and it was not long after this that they faced eviction. The Bank exercising their rights to take possession.

There is more to this, which we elaborate on in our

STOP-BREATHE-REMEMBER IN LIFE THERE IS ONLY ONE THING THAT IS CERTAIN, AND THAT IS YOU WILL DIE ONE DAY – DO NOT PANIC BECAUSE THAT IS WHEN YOU WILL MAKE A MISTAKE, DUE TO THE PRESSURES OF OTHERS.

You do not need to sign a Deed of Forbearance and it is not compulsory; you can call the Financial Council for free advice if all else fails.

"There is always something that is Do Able in every situation"…MC

This matter was resolved with a successful result because after understanding that the lawyers refused to review the application that was completed by the friendly banker. A clear indication that Sharon did not sign it with any understanding of what she was agreeing to and she did not declare the income stated. It was a battle so don't think it was this simple!). We obtained the true valuation that clearly stated the real value of the home and not the value stated on the front page of the contract. A common practice (I experienced this in the Gold Coast, which is another Beast with different regulations) that was used, the issue we face today is that the banks are well aware that the

Boom has caused homes to be overpriced with many auctions reaching way above market reserve. They have continued to Lend in the same "prudent" way, knowing that the true valuation is nowhere near the sale price.

We were able to show the actions of the banker were bordering on coercion and maladministration by the bank ... a happy ending that was overshadowed by a miscarriage. A cost incurred that is rarely considered as damages. Goliath does not experience or witness the trauma inflicted by the actions of their employees

The regulating bodies all side together and no one stands up for what is right. If it were any other business, would it get away with these tactics? Probably NOT!

Review of this Code – How many more enquires and how much more emotional turmoil

8.1. The Code states that it shall be reviewed every 3 years or sooner and it will take the *ABA to commission an independent and transparent review of this Code with the review to be conducted in consultation with:*

(a) **Banks;** who are the ones that are meant to adopt this **Code;**

(b)   *Consumer organisations;* who are they? Are they Bankers or representatives of the Bank?

The customers should have a huge say in these procedures. There is no point taking out a survey of wealthy players within the bank for customer feedback. Those who have truly been wronged by a Banker, are they commissioned to review how their lives have been impacted? The concern is that even those that have a healthy bank balance are being ripped off, they just don't feel it immediately as they are not coming from a place of 'lack'

Scenario: A customer had a deposit of over $600,000 from proceeds of a property sale. The funds went into their standard cheque account not a saving account and not earning interest benefits at all.

No one calls them regardless of the complaint raised after almost a year!

A Long standing customer never changing their banking options but had always had loans, credit card facilities and no savings, until now.

How s it that not one person called to make the customers money work for them rather than incur the account keeping fees and that is about all. We know that a banker is quick to sign you up for a loan (regardless of your ability to repay) but not in this instance!

An independent team of consultants should be commissioned to keep the Banks honest and ethical in all procedures of Banking.

(c)   The code continues to say they will also have other interested industry associations, regulatory bodies, and interested stakeholders as part of this review.

(d)   Is it only a few of us who see something wrong with this? Given the patterns of behaviour and the many tragedies that have occurred, is it not about time to come clean and just admit that the Banks need a complete overhaul? And this would not be just a simple review to be perceived as doing the right thing when clearly for centuries the wrong thing has been allowed.

8.2   It is pointless to spend so much money trying to undo what has been done and continues to cause so much pain because the Government and the Law have accepted the abuse that has been inflicted by the employees of the Banks (Businesses).

All the Employers have been questioned and they have had the advantage of receiving the content of the day's enquiry (a run sheet) so they can have the many internal advisors prepare the responses.

I'm guessing this is part of the commissioned reviews.

8.3 *You can find so much information on the websites of many regulators, but where do you go for assistance when no one wants to know?*

There are a number of regulatory bodies and many free services that all claim to provide protection to the consumer; the issue we have is that ultimately the Codes are a guideline only. To date we have not had any power to make the Employers (Banks) accountable for the actions of their employees (BAD APPLES) who have continued to inflict their own procedures on unsuspecting customers.

The Codes, Policies, and Procedures can be reviewed weekly, but that will not guarantee that past actions will stop, nor will it undo the documents that are used. The ones which allow unconscionable conduct, misleading, and fraudulent actives to be undiscovered.

SCENARIO: A family-run business that has now expanded seeks funding from a bank that the entire family has used for more than 2 generations. The relationship is a very friendly one and each week the banker comes to the family Deli and Giovanni (alias) gives the banker his weekly supply of groceries. In this small suburb everyone knows one another and as a grocer Giovanni was very popular.

In passing, Giovanni tells the banker of his plans to expand the business with his son, and with his extremely broken English agrees to meet the banker for dinner to discuss it further. Now dinner was not out of the ordinary for some bankers, especially when seeking new business. (A practice that was common for many bankers/brokers - the boys club of finance) So Giovanni has his son come along a 19-year- old who really had no interest in the family business, but it was a simple solution.

It was agreed at dinner that in order for Giovanni to be considered, he would need a different accountant, a larger firm was necessary. Giovanni's business dealt with a lot of cash sales and over the years the old man had accumulated a number of properties. It was these properties that were to be developed into childcare facilities. The banker was excited and the son did most of the translation. What is important here is that 3 of these sites were unencumbered and the only debt that remained was on the family home, but very minimal. Giovanni wanted to retire in the next five years and was already 68 years of age, his health was not the best and he wanted to return to his homeland in Italy to live out his final years with his wife.

The next few weeks the banker was constantly at the Deli, on the phone and speaking with both Giovanni and his son. During this time, they moved accountants on the advice of the banker (who gave 2 options conveniently). It was all getting too much for the old man because he had to tell his long-standing family accountant that he could not use him any longer. He was expanding! This was a dream come true and a massive achievement for a migrant with minimal education but a strong work ethic and morals. Finally his family would not have to continue to work as hard as he had all those years. Due to the ongoing pressures it was advised that the son be granted a POA (Power of Attorney) because the old man was worn down and too confused with all that needed to occur. He did things *the old school way, still writing notes on the back of envelopes and things, my word is my word mentality.*

The letter of offer was sent and the son went to a family friend to witness the signatures of both the father and the son. Documents were executed and planning began for a childcare facility, all the numbers stacked up and everything was going smoothly. During this time the father was called overseas because his mother was ill. The son had a POA and all would carry on with the friendly banker looking after things, "Do not worry, my friend!" were the parting words. The father was previously removed as a Director (he was advised after the fact!) as the son continued the business expansions and the daily running of staff and the business.

A few weeks later, the facility was up for renewal because it was structured in a way where financials were to be provided on the bank's request? Remember the new accountant? (Recommended by the Banker?) Well, it was like pulling teeth to get the documents sent over, suddenly the emails were not all that friendly and then a valuer was engaged on the bank's behalf. This now, 20-year-old was in over his head as the accountant introduces a consultant who is also a broker and deals with property acquisitions. Yet the accountant did not provide the financials that created the opportunity for the Banker to enforce internal practices and procedures and exercise their rights.

The notices kept coming, no hardship or support was offered, only confirmation by the **friendly banker that all is still ok**, *prior to the notices of default and demand. "Sign this deed of forbearance" was the advice given and not long after a receiver was appointed. The Deli was making a decent amount of cash sales and the facilities were paid, there had never been a missed or late payment.*

So what happened?

The facility was written up in such a way that certain requirements had to be satisfied or this would cause a breach. All this was nearing the time of expiration of the facility also. The new accountant failed the family **(this never happened with the previous accountant, who established the fathers business many decades ago!)**

The Receiver who was appointed also known

to the accountant, business consultant and banker, did nothing to act in the interest of the customer and attempt to work through the situation. Various solutions were proposed on many occasions but ignored or rejected., Stock was sold for hardly any monetary value, with the actual receivers taking a lot of stock (the finest foods and the best olive oil) this was witnessed by a nosey neighbor(every suburb has a few and thank God for her!). So now they locked everyone out and it didn't take long before properties were sold and documents were lost!

Fortunately, a staff member (also a relative) kept an electronic copy of everything!

When the figures were provided to ASIC as part of the general notification by the Receiver many of the figures did not coincide however ASIC did not listen to the complaints or the requests for disclosure.

The unfairness continued as the lives of this family was now being thrown away while others profited.

TIP: "With financial documents (even notes on serviettes) keep it stored away in a safe place. This is the only time to be a Hoarder"

Take a safety snap and store it on your phone but keep a record to avoid the here say!

The properties were sold for much less than the true value and the sale was arranged through the Adviser who was advising the son (getting paid handsomely, of course).

No, it wasn't sold back to the family as a tactic or last resort to salvage anything! This particular family migrated to Australia in the 70s and worked hard in their new country, paid sufficient taxes, and helped everyone in the community. The properties were sold to a company specially set up for the Childcare facilities and were also previous clients of the Adviser. (I discovered later)

The entire family was bankrupted under the rights of the Lender and the documentation, another great way to stop customers seeking answers and defending themselves. (Destroying their identity) Prior to the Bankruptcy, they did seek legal assistance whilst they could afford to, and then out of desperation held onto hope that others were ethical and would act with integrity. The son sought the help of another advisor, a broker with another bank. A friendly solicitor introduces this man, who is informed of the situation, understands that that the father is away and believes all is ok. He tells the son that he is unable to get the facility quick enough but he can help as long as he has the father's POA! The Broker gets a loan in the father's name through a reputable bank!! Now it gets even more problematic; the father is unaware. The money is spent on lawyers presuming to investigate; however, due to the executed documentation and the highly experienced legal brigade of the Banks, the judge rules against the family. Now all is lost.

But they had their home (which they managed to pay off during the planning stages), except the money stopped and for the first time the family had to go on welfare. Soon the banks sent out demands and the son panicked. They were being evicted and had nowhere to turn because in this humble home lived not only the immediate family but also the aunt and uncle. No one looked at their story and no one heard it from the onset, everyone focuses on the more recent activity and not the lead up to the situation.

We stopped the evection and mediated a result; the family remains in the home and the father continues to live in his homeland. The outcome was a win/win for all concerned, *especially for the son who deals with mental illness from the entire trauma. After working most of his life in Australia the father still has his home and the legal team that represented the Bank are known to be ruthless. It's not Impossible to reach a **'fair'** outcome.*

The simple story is that in this matter the issue was the Broker and his relationship within the bank allowed him to manipulate the system and provide a fraudulent loan to a very desperate customer. "Desperation makes us Vulnerable"

The questions for which I sought answers were based on prudential lending practices and the overall credit approval process; having had the customer (Son) there to face up to his responsibility also and elaborate on the actions between the Broker/Banker. It was a fair outcome for all. But this all could have progressed to the standard processes. A default was previously sent and a default judgment passed by the courts, (reliant of the documents provided by the Banks and ultimately their Lawyers with all that was necessary), possession the next step, and then sale of assets. Ultimately Bankruptcy for the balance of the debt in its entirety and the rest is history.

Principal & default interest plus costs, so technically the banks do not actually lose, or do they?

This is difficult to avoid and no amount of rewording the regulations and codes will ensure they are followed due to the overall of systemic procedures. We are dealing with documentation designed to protect the risk of the Banks (your money theoretically), their exposure to Risk and the interest of the shareholders.

The UGLY TRUTH- there is nothing in place to protect 'YOU' from the Person encouraging you to sign a facility that guarantees the banker or their associates the incentive of either monetary or job promotion as a reward. There is no recourse for unethical behaviour only redundancy and the ability to move on to another Banking institution to do it all over again. This time their tactics are refined so that they do not get caught again. No matter what it's a Loose/Loose situation for the unsuspecting customer.

"WE ARE DEALING WITH HUMANS NOT ROBOTS!"... MC

There is not much on any website where you

will find what to do when it all turns to S.H.I.T - (Suddenly Heading Into Trouble).

The information provided is of little use or benefit after the fact! Yes, the websites provide information and it all sounds as though it may *help*, but not in all cases. The less complicated matters have been resolved apparently, but too many find themselves on an *emotional rollercoaster* ride. These issues have been the various cases where ASIC or other regulators have identified issues with fees and interest etc....not the individuals.

Just as you get on the ride and read all you think you need to know according to your circumstances, you are fairly ok at this point. Then you call up only to discover that your situation does not fall into the many rules of abled support or the compensative amounts so you are on your own.

Now you are heading down the roller coaster at an incredible rate, fear and panic sets in. You listen to whomever is willing to listen to your frustrations, as you seek to get off this ride, it was not the experience you signed up for!

You then try one of the other alternatives, even approaching the same banker; again we are riddled with emotions that cloud our judgment. You are in a panic state due to the demand and other notification that are now served and the date for deadlines are nearing. So you buckle up as you make your complaint to FOS, ASIC, ABA, APRA, CIO, even the ATO. Along with paying an expert with money you don't have. You feel a sense of temporary relief as the ride beings to climb up to the top; you're in with a chance to defend yourself from these unexplainable events.

As the relief builds and you think, "This isn't so bad." the ride on the way up appears to be easy ... nothing to be afraid of anymore! The date of doom is nearing and you are told once again you have no more options but to find the money to repay or simply allow the Banks to exercise their rights because legally...you signed the agreement and nothing you believed to be true was noted on your file! Now you have also lost the money and time, that could have helped you live instead (hypothetically speaking) You then come racing down so quickly that your face feels like it is going to peel off. A Rollercoaster many of us have experienced.

The Codes of Practice or any other policy becomes irrelevant when you are facing internal procedures that you allow by signing the agreements drafted by the banks' legal teams.

Much of the management staff are in fact Lawyers' so you are talking to a person well versed in the law and they know best how to manipulate it for their own protection. Whilst representing yourself innocently believing in the system and professionalism of the organization. One major deceit that occurs in a many cases' and in my own experience is the team where your file is conveniently moved, are the ones that ultimately have the power to destroy you without recourse. This department, Asset Management (Risk Management), which usually receives all your files once passed on by your friendly banker, never really explains what they're all about.

> *"Warning" – If you are not informed be on guard and wary of what they are saying and promising. You should always know who and what department is taking action- Diva Tip*

Customers will attend these introduction meetings alone to see the new banker who "*took over my file*" (the usual story from many victims) without taking a professional representative with them, **and you should!** In a number of matters, the same two people dealt with 4 particular matters during the same period. Not once was it disclosed that they actually came from an Insolvency background.

SCENARIO: John and his company's file was moved to this particular Department, except it was also moved to another state. The expiation he received from his friendly (Business partner-like) banker was that it was to be moved to Queensland where the properties (Assets) were. John had previously only dealt with the Queensland branch of another Bank, but his initial banker was from Sydney. , So when his file was moved he did not question it. The problem here was that John had no idea that this was actually the END! His file was moved to Credit Asset Management in Queensland.

His friendly new bankers (BAD APPLES) all came from an insolvency background, working in the bank's risk management. However, they never introduced themselves or explained what the actual department involvement would be... Death Row for

The duo claimed to be there to assist (help), so John was still very optimistic as he displayed the project's potential. You see, John had essentially completed a whole development and had a potential site that was a "no brainer" (easily achieved) project. His main issue was that the Broker (ex-banker) coerced John into a well-planned incestuous arrangement with the assistance of a banker he'd worked with at his previous Bank.

This is already an oxidization situation (they were riddled with fungus carried forward from the orchard which they came. Like any harvest, if the flesh is opened up and the oxygen (temptation & greed) penetrates the flesh, it is compromised and rots!

Environment factors affect how quickly the fruit rots. The documents and systems conceal the behaviour of greedy bankers (power or money temptation). Apples require light to ripen; fungi (concealed behaviour) do not! There for Light that isn't supplemented by heat (exposure) won't hasten the rotting, it will only allow it to survive longer!

If we continue to talk and provide media exposure or more costly inquiries, it will not eliminate the rotten behaviour unless these people are punished. It is not just about creating monetary fines for banks (which customers generally pay for anyway). These activities have been perpetrated for centuries, unless we change the culture of how these actions are penalized we will not create Change!

That is how simple it is.

Unfortunately we cannot enforce a new legislation that is governed by a . We punish people who mistreat animals yet we treat other people/families inhumanely. Allowing Bad apples to enrich themselves by manipulation, fraud and theft while continuing to torment and disbelieve victims.

Persecuting the victim allows widespread Abuse to continue within the Banking culture.

We face a bigger evil and that is that Brokers are not regulated properly and if they team up with a BAD APPLE they can leave an epidemic of destruction while working under the Banks license. Just another way to get around the regulations.

Humans with underhanded motives are abled enough to find the loopholes in legislation and law when they have never been made accountable for their actions.

In one particular meeting of discovery, a very well respected senior manager said that if only 1 % of the 50-odd thousand employees were BAD APPLES, then they were doing well!

If I calculate 1% of the $15 billion dollar profits recorded for the first half of the year, that's only a fraction of what Brokers and Bankers earn by abusing their position of power and their customers. Establishment fees can vary from $30,000 to $100s of thousands not to mention the supposed arms length sales of assets in conjunction with friendly Receivers. Many senior bankers have a tonne of assets in family trusts built up this way.

These are never disclosed and when these fees were disputed, all the regulatory bodies confirmed that apparently this was allowed. Has the system gone out of control and now Bad Apples were unstoppable? ... legalising the criminal actions of any human being abled to carry out temptation of greed and or power.

I actually corrected that figure based on the people I've helped, and that is nothing in the scheme of things. So it was more like 25% but even that 1% meant their Orchard was infested regardless.

So back to the terms and conditions: what good are they anyway when not everything is disclosed?

There is no pesticide to eradicate this fungus, so the next best thing for the farmer to do is to deny that his harvest is bad, especially to the regulators and then blame his customers! His business associates; advisors, accountants, and legal representatives now need to conform because they have recently been made aware of the possible spread of disease to their customers. This epidemic could cause major problems even though they are funding most of the regulating bodies anyway. It may cause an economic disaster if these inquiries continue, which they make very public during question time.

PART C: DISCLOSURES are MORE LIKE NONDISCLOSURE

9.   Terms and conditions

9.1.   **We** will expeditiously provide to **you**, or any person, on request: the **terms and conditions** of any ongoing **banking service** we currently offer; full particulars of **standard fees and charges** that are, or may become, payable for any **banking service we** currently offer; and particulars of the interest rates applicable to any **banking service we** currently offer.

The words above are directly from the Code of Practices and I touched on this earlier in the book … it is wrong to have the statement as "we will quickly (in other words) provide you!" Terms and conditions are one of the first things mentioned when it comes to disputing or questioning any facility. "It's in your clients terms and conditions," one of the first statements from a legal representative! The problem many have faced is that they never received these pretty looking pamphlets or booklets. If you have used a Broker, you may never ever see them as the Banker had sent them directly to the Broker and you only ever receive what the Broker had passed on.

Shouldn't this be a mandatory obligation and not one you have to request, considering them to be binding documents with your acceptance of the facility?

What happens when fees are not disclosed (and believe me they aren't always)?

Do you notice them amongst the words that are sometimes ambiguously written?

Can we rewrite our mortgage documents?

Many of these questions have answers with viable solutions, proven by the recent results!

9.2. The **terms and conditions** of **our banking services** will:

(a) Be distinguishable from marketing or promotional material;

This is definitely not the case with many products, especially credit cards, home loans and virtually all facilities. If you are given the terms and conditions, do you really read them or do you ignore the pamphlets and only file away the documents or like many others…throw them away?

(b) Be in English and any other language **we** consider to be appropriate;

So are these explained correctly to speaking and non-speaking customers?

By English do they mean in everyday terminology or do we all need university degrees? Regardless you may need an interpreter.

(c)   <u>Be consistent with this **Code**</u>.

This I have to debate, given that the Code is only a guide and all these obligations have been breached in the many cases now resolved!

(d)   <u>Be provided at the time of or before the contract for an ongoing **banking service** is made, except where it is impracticable to do so, in which case they will be provided as soon as practicable afterward;</u> and this, in itself, is confusing. Is it trying to say that you really need to read the terms and conditions before you sign or that they are irrelevant and it's ok to receive them afterward? Who makes sure you actually read it and understand it?

This is why it is your responsibility to take control of your LIFE ... because they will pass on that responsibility regardless of the circumstances.

(e) Draw attention to the availability of the general descriptive information referred to in clauses 13.1 and 13.2 if it is relevant and will specifically mention the availability of information about:

I thought it was only me who did not have these clauses explained, but neither did others; so, who determines when they are relevant?

Why do Bankers mislead you by simplifying the terms & Conditions and all the obviously relevant clauses? Instead we usually hear that "these are all the standard clauses, not much to worry about" (or words to that effect)

(i) Account opening procedures;

Does general descriptive information about Account opening also explain that a Bank may take your money if it is in crisis and due to their obligations. In other words they may take your deposited funds. It happened in the UK, USA, and Europe, and now Australia. It's called Bail-In.

(ii) **Our** obligations regarding the confidentiality of **your** information;

Given the Banks position they should have a Duty of Care to 'Act with care and Diligence, Duty to Act in good faith & Duty to NOT improperly use position (All noted in the Corporations Act) The documents do not explain what rights you have when a Banker has used your private information for their personal gain. It also has no mention of the Banker's responsibility to be transparent with your information. It is a GUIDE only. You have no proof of what the Banker has noted on your internal files and ultimately they can override the internal system at any given time without your knowledge.

No Bank has actually disclosed how they police this issue and how they are alerted when the information has been amended. Is there a supervisor or internal authorization perhaps?

There should be but we have not had the privilege to date; however in many cases the senior relationship bankers were the usual suspects that make it even harder to disprove given their position and status.

Generally a director or other officers of a corporation commits an offence if they are:

- Reckless *(allowing misconduct to continue and not taking action to rectify the situations known of)*

- Intentionally dishonest *(I haven't met a Bad Apple that confesses to his manipulation & fraud)* and fail to exercise their powers and discharge their duties. *(To resign and allow others to camouflage your retirement in other words!)*

- In good faith in the best interest of the corporation; or for Proper Purpose?? (Do directors of banking institutions turn a blind eye to the deceit and misconduct to maintain their exorbitant salaries and bonuses whilst increasing profits and share prices that do not truly reflect the corporation's activities?) Banking was suppose to be a secure organization that assisted you with your financial future not to ensure you fail.

Many other laws apply but for this purpose we are focusing on the ASIC regulations for Directors and Office holders in general. Sadly Bank directors appear to be excluded from the disciplinary actions of 'standard business'

The above carries penalties that include jail time and in many cases, (especially during 2008 -2011) the customer that was deceived by who I call the usual suspects. Many people have lost everything and sadly some lost their lives leaving behind grieving families, because of the carefully designed tactics of some. The punishment for attempted manslaughter (attempting to destroy (kill) a person) only applies to a physical attack; this abuse is subtle and just as deadly. The difference is that no one acknowledges the criminal element.

(iii)   Complaint handling procedures;

This is difficult when your complaint is about the actions of your banker. Sadly, the procedure for complaints handling is usually after you are too far-gone and in hardship.

We are more reluctant to make our concerns know whilst a facility is about to be granted or recently executed. As soon as you feel or experience that your banker is acting unethically you should report it..

"Two (2) Wrongs don't make a Right, it

will show that you were part of the
manipulation and now unhappy!"

> *The information provided to them.*
> *Surely a Director must act upon the*
> *negligence of his employees?*

Note: I AM NOT A LAWYER – thank GOD
because I would not have been able to negotiate
the outcomes to date. It is all about Common
Sense that is misconstrued amongst Lawyers,
usually from the either side.

(iv) Bank Cheques; NO major issues –more
detailed description regarding digital payment
is needed since Cheques are old school!

> *Diva Tip: You should make a written*
> *complaint even if nothing is done.*
> *Under the Governance & Conduct of*
> *the Bank, the Director is reliant on*

(v) The advisability of **you** informing **us**
promptly when **you** are in financial difficulty;
Many times you are reliant on your banker for
this because most customers tell their banker

everything and it should be the banker's obligation to offer assistance. Surprisingly many people are not aware or confident enough to approach the Bank with Hardship. There is always that element of fear of being defaulted and creating more problems for yourself, so many are reluctant. A Broker will only try to refinance you from another Bank increasing their revenue opportunity.

The Bank should not reprimand you in any way regarding a change in circumstances, LIFE happens and we cannot always control certain events that occur. It is obligated to assist you and not place you in further hardship. Nor should it place you in a position where you will jeopardize your financial livelihood.

However, in a majority of cases, it's all too late, many have literally kicked themselves for listening to others and attempting to reach out to the Bank. So, if you tell the banker of your change in circumstances, he should assist you and not cause more hardship. Get it in writing and record conversations for the 'what if, scenarios'

If a Banker is a Bad Apple you are at their mercy because even if you call the call center (customer care) they will redirect you to your Banker. This is frustrating when you finally realize that they are the ones that are harming you.

(vi) The advisability of **you** reading the **terms and conditions** applying to the relevant **banking service**.

Again, in all cases this rarely happens and in fact a number of matters involved a Broker and Introducer who would receive the documents first.

9.3. Any written **terms and conditions** will include a statement to the effect that the relevant provisions of this **Code** apply to the **banking service** but need not set out those provisions.

What does this mean? That the terms and conditions will say that relevant requirement of the code apply to the banking service but need not establish those requirements?

The statement is confusing enough; simply, *The Banker can do as they please*!

SCENARIO: At a mediation where the facility was arranged by a Broker and the Banker, the customer did not receive these terms and conditions mentioned. The problem; during a mediation the Bank's representative said, "It's in your terms and conditions, they were sent to you!" 'No' they weren't, they were actually sent to the Broker's address and were never passed on to the customer. However the customer was to depend on them! They are a document relied upon in a dispute but not fully explained. Once the point was proven and I could demonstrate that when the facility was renewed, without the customer ever seeing the terms and condition, we won the argument. (Clearly demonstrating the inconsistency of the Bankers declaration) noting that the address on the initial facility was to the Broker and thereafter to the customer's address. This raised the question of integrity, ethics and the ability to manipulate the internal data entry.

Diva Tip: Make sure: You 'must have' a copy of every document you sign

9.4 **We** will include (where relevant) the following in or with our **terms and conditions** applying to a **banking service:**

The following clauses are also written to confuse and make no sense, especially

common sense, as many bankers break all the guidelines without detection! It's all a bit too late when things don't go as promised.

The Code states that the bank will disclose standard fees and charges that apply to the facility:

This needs to be elaborated; the disclosure must provide details of all the inclusions, undisclosed agreements with introducers and brokers alike. All third parties! Remember if fees are added to your facility you will be paying a lot more than stated.

SCENARIO: Joe's Broker introduced him to a banker who then followed through with an application. However, Joe never sighted this document and all details were discussed with the Broker. Joe did receive a document that outlined an establishment fee of $85,000, of which $15,000 was due and payable upon the initiation of the applications. On application meant a query relating to credit acceptance? If you paid the money were you certain to get the loan approved?

Joe, at this point, was desperate because time had passed and he had to refinance. What do you think Joe did?

"That's right, what we all generally do ... sign and send back ... the rest of the fee is added to the loan ... so it will be ok, I will get approved and work harder to repay it, typical justification thoughts... Right? We are almost too PREDICTABLE or are we coerced into the same familiar patterns of behaviour that the Bad Apples have mastered?"

The issue with this is that the fee was not explained and that half of it was going to the Broker. At no stage did the Broker disclose this either; and, to add more salt to the wound, he was being paid separately by Joe. There was an initial fee that was paid up front! These Bad Apples worked together on a number of customers in the same manner and during the same period. Somehow they still remain in the infested orchard, surviving within the boundaries of the Banking System and promoted to even greater positions of power.

The various clauses of the Codes continue to state that all interest charges are explained in full terms and conditions that are provided. Not to mention any changes would be in writing.

Ugly Truth: *You expect the Banker to act in good faith and abide by the implied terms of the code, however that is difficult to argue when your banker has another agenda. Unfortunately the actions of a dishonest person can and usually are camouflaged by the executed document and the systems surrounding them. Regardless of the statement suggesting you will be notified at all times. It has a very broad meaning...to act in good faith. In many cases the parties involved have a long term rational when agreeing to sign an agreement that ultimately differed to the initial explanation by a trusting person in a position of power.*

WARNING: Document every conversation as implied actions (even if they are carried out) do not form part of the written contract and it is a rarity for a banker to follow up his promised actions in writing.

However many more guidelines that the Bankers are to adhere to can and are usually overlooked. The Banker and Broker who work together will always protect each other and it will always become your word against theirs.

DIVA NTK (Need To Know) – It is important to completely understand what you are signing up for and you have a right to question anything. It's Your Future and it will clarify things for both parties. The Bank also needs to be aware of their employees promising one things and doing another. In the scenarios where you have turned to a Bad Apple out of desperation, NTK – you will be thrown out when that banker decides he wants you to and everything has an expiry date!

SCENARIO: Joe was not informed of changes to his interest until after it had occurred. What he signed up for allowed the Banks to change things to their liking or appetite, as they say, without notice. (A general term in most agreements) Joe thought because his friendly Banker (introduced by his trusting Broker) said he would look after him and be there for him, that he was in safe hands. These Bad Apples made a rotten apple pie with his file. The Banking system was the fan forced oven that baked it!

In Joe's matter, regardless that his banker was aware of his situation at all times, had him execute an agreement that he had promised would not be 'a problem. The interest imposed and the demands of the "credit" department were impossible to adhere to in the timeframe provided. The

Broker constructed the facility with the Banker and the terms only explained upon signing of the documentation. Joe did what we would all generally do in his position and signed. Believing the promises made by the banker saying he would look after 'Joe and his family' was the only way possible in order to get the loan approved! A term/pattern many bankers rely on (like good cop, bad cop between Brokers and Bankers), you see I found it so convenient when the banker gave that excuse, given that he was responsible for getting the facility through to credit. Your banker should never overburden you, making certain that you were not going to fail in the first place, given he should be aware of credit criteria. His duty is to be Risk adverse not exploit his position and constructed destine to fail facility. In all cases, the burden is handed back to the "credit department," allowing the Bad Apples to cover up their own actions. Concealing his deceit so he can continue to be perceived as your friendly banker. Sadly, you have no idea what is actually on your file notes internally, unless the Apple is a Pink Lady (type of Apple only) and is honoring her position. The good employee is willing to disclose their actions to you. Otherwise there is no transparency, as discovered in Joe's case.

(Cheques are hardly used anymore), some of the more irrelevant procedure are included, but all amounting to the fact that majority of the Codes do not assist you when the Bank decides it does not want your business any longer. They have a legal right to do so at any given time. You allow it by signing.

That is why bankers can abuse you, it is a necessity for your future endeavor and that makes you susceptible.

*It does not explain the concerns you will face when this occurs and it may not happen overnight but it can happen. A harvest does not ripen overnight; it takes time. The Banker can get rid of your file easily over time, the hard part was convincing you that he has given you the best and only option. However, it is difficult to get rid of a Banker who has all the tools he needs to appear his job was completed within the **guidelines, turning you into a disgruntled customer.***

"This comment is brought about from the numerous cases who had turned to various

lawyers and regulators that all concluded 'the banks were within their rights.' A discerning realization on the customer that did nothing wrong but 'trusted' a professional with their financial FUTURE."

<u>The Code</u> *goes into the guidelines of term deposits and interest payments; the simple explanation is that the Bank is a business, one that uses our money. The bank invests and maximizes its return, while rewarding us with a minimal reward for using money that wasn't theirs. However, if you need to break that term due to your situation, then there is a fee involved, so they make money regardless.*

We have a massive problem when it comes to understanding the many Codes of Practice, Procedures and simply conduct. There are many regulations however not much success in defending yourself after the intentional actions of an employee that is availed with the ability and opportunity to silence the innocent. The perpetrator is protected by the system and the victim continues to be victimized by the arrogance of management and the need to appear ethical to retain community trust.

BANKING IS SIMPLY ANOTHER FOR PROFIT BUSINESS

A Bank is simply another business that makes enormous profits and pays exorbitant salaries to management that is focused on creating best possible profits and dividends for shareholders. The difference is that they are able to use everyone's and anyone's money to do so. It is apparent that the Banks have a complete support system of everyone so how can this business fail?

Perhaps we all need to rethink business and consider;

- Finding a business using other people's money,
- Charging interest on that money,
- Lending out someone else's money, without consideration to their Risk
- Creating currency with no asset,
- Take all the risk you want, knowing you have insurance if it fails (you will be Bailed Out regardless of whose money it is)
- Utilize the Tax system to your advantage
- Benefit from your Bad debt or Bad choices
- Never be accountable for any of the activates within your business
- Earn great rewards for doing SO

If we are all governed by the same Regulatory Bodies, why do some Directors and Business owners get away with rogue activities? There are many more cases involving ASIC matters in relation to Company dealings that clearly demonstrate the problems we face with manipulation of the system, but the Banks are in a league of their own. Many regulatory organisations continue to turn a blind eye and pretend to listen however do not investigate. Majority of the cases would result in prevention of tax evasion and defrauding other creditors and theft, basically. (Families losing their livelihoods due to dishonest conduct)

But they cannot investigate although they decide to keep your complaint on record for future investigations…what does that mean?

They will investigate when they feel pressured to or when it affect someone they know?

Someone who is high profile?

Which one of these multiple choice answers?

If you were a director of a business and it was clearly failing, that would be insolvent trading, yet a Bank is told to STOP further activities by their parent company, because it is facing collapse isn't classified as insolvent! Even with no future funding this bank continued to be bullish in their activities to fund without consideration to the capital held. Even with NO further funding it continued business involving further indebtedness and more aggressive approaches because a larger bank would buy it out.

> *"When I raised this point it was a sore spot and dismissed by senior management."*

Even with NO further funding it continued business involving further indebtedness and more aggressive approaches because a larger bank would buy them out. What's worse, the temptation was greater for Bad Apples to deceive on a larger scale while earning benefits and generating an even bigger loan book and also lining their pockets and their employers.

This was explained to me as not being the case, so I did some more investigating, and it was the case! The simplest explanation is that any transactions during this period should not have occurred under the instructions of the Parent company. So, the management of the company (Director) would be personally liable, if it was any other entity and wasn't a Bank. This strategic move was beneficial to the new owner because this new owner was not bound by existing agreements, they would be null and void. The new owner was also licensed with a Basel One license, with a different criteria altogether. Appearances had to be kept up so management did not impose changes to the current practices and procedure of the second tier lender (many went to this bank through relationships between, accountants, brokers & bankers) but they seem to be followed regardless. There are certain criteria that have to be upheld when you are a tier one lender and one of the 'Big Four.'

Then you have the responsibility of staffing, you are liable for the actions of your employees and have insurances in place to mitigate your losses. A Bank should be the same however they have more than just money to lose. Their losses are generally covered anyway.

If you, as a director, hired someone and he/she caused injury or some form of injustice, you are responsible as the employer. There is no recourse for a banker; a protected species and sadly all the Board members can choose to ignore any wrong doing, even when the responsibility should be with the Directors.

If you are negligent as a Director and then continue to cover up those actions, you are personally responsible … my goodness, you may even face criminal charges.

SCENARIO: If you entice people to invest their money into a scheme that is based on exaggeration, when you are fully aware that the risk potential is high and there, you have defrauded them into parting with their money. Isn't that criminal?

There are cases of which we are all aware: Landmark, Storm, and others, where the Banks were heavily involved. How is this different from the individual Directors who gain funds from individuals for a concept only it is destined to fail? – Too many Bad Apples.

In one ASIC matter, an individual decided to open up several businesses and in each of these a concept was written up with a false sense of security provided by an exaggerated ROI (return on investment). Shareholders provided money, yet nothing was done other than a company set up and then deregistered. There was only an email address and website and that was the business; people lost money. You may think "why" would you invest in such a thing? 'I wouldn't', but you do because of the promise and gain you were supposedly to receive. It is the emotional rollercoaster you experience as people play with your emotions without you realizing and it is easy to fall for an offer of potential financial gain. After a number of these businesses were reported, ASIC finally acted, with police involvement for fraudulently obtaining a monetary gain. We cannot keep up with the amount of creative scamming schemes that target the innocent. The directors found guilty went to jail, insider trading is also a jail term but Banks get away with this daily.

Then you have the Phoenix arrangements to defraud creditors (usually the tax man), many companies will generate millions of dollars of debt and act on the advice of a creative professional to Liquidate that company in time. Then creating another entity to continue the lifestyle and previous operations. There are so many evidenced matters where this had occurred and depending on the situation the director becomes a chameleon (Shadow director). This is to continue defrauding the creditors until the air is clear and the only ones affected by the collateral damage is the creditors (taxpayers also lose)

What is worse is that there are many situations these Directors have been assisted by creative Bad Apples within the Banks. These Bad Apples are actually defrauding other Banks and on a number of occasions had moved into management roles within the Bank they deceived! There is no loyalty so I'd be worried if I was a rough director that relied on this connection, a Bad Apple will not leave a paper trail but will always protect himself before others.

"DESPERATE PEOPLE DO DESPERATE THINGS!"

"WHY DO THE RIGHT THING, WHEN SO MANY THAT HAVE CLEARLY DONE THE WRONG THING CONTINUE TO GET AWAY WITH IT, WHILE WE SUFFER!" – A REGULAR STATEMENT BY MANY.

SO how is it any different to what has happened in Banking? A director is still at the helm of the activities, but he is not responsible for ensuring that nothing untoward is going on. He continues to deny any wrongdoing and is allowed to proceed without remorse for the many lives that are affected by his ignorance to the conduct of employees in a position of power.

If we truly consider that a Bank who employs the best consultants, lawyers, and economists should be more astute when it comes to the markets, property, agribusiness and the economy as a whole. Why are we continuing the same cycles as the past without breaking them? Having the same conversations year after year enquires and amended legislations when it hasn't changed anything really?

So why are the directors of our Banks allowed to place us in a vulnerable position when they know how to prevent your personal financial death?

Because they can! If there were penalties they would think twice like all of us. The truth is that even ASIC or others cannot or will not punish these actions, there is more of an incentive to cover up the Bad Apples that to disclose them.

THE CODE continues to explain what the banks' guidelines will be for Credit Cards, deposit taking, withdrawals, account functions, and the other entire BS; (bastardized system) but it isn't BS, it is Basic Standards that are usually breeched. Once you question the Banker, however, then that is where the codes, terms and conditions become important and very relevant not simply a guideline.

When you continue through to the part where it actually explains - in case of an electronic dispute, you only have a certain time frame to report. For all the astute Banking customer who check their statements regularly, making sure that nothing irregular has occurred, well you will report any discrepancies immediately. (So much respect and hats off to you if you have managed to keep the banks accountable) Many (including yours truly) get too caught up with LIFE and it is all about finding the time. BUT YOU HAVE TO DO THIS! It is because of LIFE and it's busy-ness that the banks have been abled to overcharge, increase rates and fee due to our complacency. Many still believe there is nothing they could do regarding fees, interest etc...

SCENARIO: A Bank is only responsible for a window of activities on your accounts regarding credit cards and a few other products. Therefore to only advise your banker may not be the best way to deal with banking issues. In case it is a Bad Apple like in Anne's matter, she worked full time and was dealing with a break up after 10 years of marriage, and had 2 small children. So life was hectic, to say the least. She had always banked with this particular Bank and her banker was aware of her personal life, including her husband's dealings. One night, after having the longest and most grueling week, she sat down and opened her mail to find that her credit card was again due. This time instead of simply looking at the payable amount due and then preceding to transfer the payment, she looked through the statement.

Anne noticed the transactions that she could not possibly have made and then discovered more transaction with smaller amounts; she immediately went online to report the queries. After making a complaint online, she decided to call her banker in the morning because the transactions stemmed back for a number of years, all unnoticed.

The Banker assured her that he would investigate the transactions, then after not hearing back she made a complaint directly to the Credit Card department; they actually said they could not go back for the entire amount. They could reimburse what had occurred for a 6 month period after their investigations, but she would need to contact MasterCard directly to discuss the remaining years of transaction. Anne was horrified as she added up the transactions. Spending hours going through the statements and now in a state of panic. After three months, it all became clear: her husband was behind all the issues with the bank.

There was one problem, however, they were separated so they had equal responsibility, but their story had a common pattern. Her husband ran a business however everything was in her name (debts really) and her signature on the documentation. The husband however had made a few changes and he appointed a liquidator to his business, declared Bankruptcy, and the Banks decided to go for Anne for the entire debt. She also discovered that she was a guarantor of a facility which she really had no idea. We managed to source documents that showed that the banker had not reported her earlier complaints and concerns. When the couple's circumstances changed they were not recorded and he (the banker) sided with the husband and assisted in removing him from various documents.

He also assisted the husband throughout the

process of repossession and demands. Leaving the frustration and fear of the unknown to Anne, through no fault of her own other than being a supportive and loving wife. This happens more times than we want to believe it does.

Anne was helped by guiding her gentle through a process I called L.I.F.E;

She could not afford lawyers and everywhere she turned promised to assist but ultimately took what little she could afford and basically said, 'Your name is on the executed documents, there is not much you can do...we may be able to assist you to look for finance, or make the bank an offer!'

Really!! That was the solution.

Time was running out, she found every piece of paper and scribble she had written, diary notes and other documentation to map out her timeline and story. After almost a month of persisting a meeting was granted and we were able to articulate the situation simply and without the emotional BS.

We mediated a resolve that was a win-win for the Bank and Anne, along with her two children. It is doable!

Plan the Divorce Before the Wedding.

I am in Love with LOVE, so do not take this comment that all weddings end in divorce and that this is a given. It is more about being RESPONSIBLE and not simply thinking of wedding bells.

Women sign with an Emotional DNA – Anne is an accountant and blamed herself for being STUPID (Stopped-Troubled-Unable-Programmed-Intimidated-Depressed), so once we went through her actual L.I.F.E, she began to realise what I always said: we allow our situation to make us feel stupid (my analogy), we are far from dumb, and no matter how many alphabets are behind your name, we are all susceptible to the influences of a person in a position of power. The feeling of violation leaves you weak and fragile in the beginning, then the inability to understand 'how' it all turns BAD!

SCENARIO; Mandy, a 24-year-old, noticed all these amounts coming from her credit card and when she finally went back into the last 2 years' worth of statements, these transactions had gone unnoticed. OMG! They added up to over $4,000, except the bank would only refund the last 6 months. She managed to get them to pay 9 months' worth, but they added up to a minor portion of the funds taken. They passed the responsibility on to

MasterCard! We then looked into the policy and the connection with MasterCard ... WOW ... what we think we know we actually don't!

The other issue that was uncovered was Mandy never should have been offered the amount the Bank increased on her card limit. She didn't even provide additional information for that process, it was as simple as saying 'yes'.

No terms and conditions provided until the new card arrived along with the glossy brochures.

> **TIP: You are expected TO read them not throw them out like junk mail because they hold the key to protecting yourself – believe it or not!**

So, rather than go through each and every clause of the Code, I decided to make mention of the ones that have been breached in many cases. However they were ignored as the overarching facility agreement is the main document that enables the Banks to have the ability to enforce their rights. There are many codes that need to be understood if you are to defend yourself from the Bad Apples amongst the Banking Orchard. Consumer Credit Law, Corporation Law, Privacy Law, Contracts Law, there are many others also. You also have the regulators, ASIC, ABA (Australian Bankers

Association, APRA, FOS and other Ombudsman services. Then with the various codes; conduct, practice and procedures I found it conflicting and confusing given the actual actions the Banks instigate. How was this even possible?

"YOU CANNOT POLICE EVERY HUMAN BEING IN A POSITION OF POWER, BUT THEN WHO DO YOU HOLD ACCOUNTABLE?"

What about the Privacy of your LIFE (Information) basically, you do not have rights to your personal information it belongs to the Bank. A Bank gives you what they want you to see; you have no rights or ability to the banker's notes and information he has placed in your file. Unless you end up in court and go through the discovery process! That is when it is a little too late.

Then as an employee of the Bank you have no idea of whom he passes that information to or how he is using it.

SCENARIO: Steve trusted his banker, who was introduced to him by his accountant. Steve is a simple man who lives a humble life and works very hard. He is a factory worker and has done so for the last 15 years. He wanted to buy an investment property and already had a mortgage on his family home. The problem Steve faced was that he was given a facility that over-extended his capacity to pay and, after disputing the matter, we discovered the original application was amended internally. Thank God Steve was a hoarder, so we could show the original as opposed to the document the Bank relied on as its internal discovery ... the banker never lost his job and still does as he has always done!

So, you cannot control a Bad Apple from spreading disease. The Banks were under no obligation to show any internal records. In other cases, they simply fall back on the timeframe and that there were no found documents in archives. "Excuses and cover-up," but it is allowed.

In many cases, the customers actually complained to FOS (Financial Ombudsman Service). When they obtained their files under the Freedom of Information's Act, the customers were shocked to discover that no actual investigation had been completed correctly.

Usually the first request for information to the Bank would be how the facility was initiated

–   The application that was submitted, loan approval documentation and the executed facility plus the latest statement to verify the indebtedness…Standard right?

Remember, I mentioned Joe; well, he never saw his application that was handled by a Broker. Steve's application was a clear case of fraud (not by him), many others were the same, yet FOS made a determination that the Bank was in the right even though they never sighted the actual application.

So how do you really get justice when there is no way of ensuring everyone is actually doing what he or she say they will do? To be fair I can totally understand the difficulty in acting on every complaint and having to investigate every allegation. However they are an organization funded to perform these tasks, they have employees that receive a weekly pay to work on these complaint as part of their job description. For many it is a job but for the multitudes of victims that have been violated by a systemic abuse of power. The emotional scarring that is unseen and another layer of disappointment when you have reached out for a glimmer of Hope and another professional let you down.

Have you ever been so adamant that you have been deceived, but no one else can see it? We all know our truth and when you defend yourself the systems in place can manipulate that truth and you become the bad guy.

What I have experienced is that they, too, can see it, but they are better off not opening that can of worms that has been contained within the boundaries of Banking.

The Code remains as the guidelines continue to be ignored, but someone can surely force the Banks to comply ... right?

In clause 9.1: under Copies of Documents, it states that the bank does not have to give you a copy of notices or other documents after termination of your facility ... So if I were a Bad Apple and saw an opportunity to make money for nothing – knowing I could get away with it, why wouldn't I?

"Remember Stranger Danger – how well do you know the person who is your banker? (You can't be sure of anything given it constantly changes)"

Yes!

> *Ugly Truth: A Bad Apple (Unethical human being) can manipulate the internal system at whim, without compulsory reporting and explanation as to why. Remember there is Good Bad and Indifferent in all of us and you can never be certain of a stranger's true motives.*

IT IS AWFULLY DIFFICULT TO PROVE 'DUTY OF CARE' (THAT SHOULD BE A MANDATORY PRACTICE FOR ALL BANKERS) WHEN ALL THE DOCUMENTS AND THE TIMING OF THE ACTIONS OF A BAD APPLE WILL SHOW THEM AS 'DOING THE RIGHT THING!'

During the GFC especially, many Bad Apples had the perfect economic climate to become money-grabbing vultures. Many Bankers took a redundancy package from their employers and then reinvented themselves as introducers to their mates;

Merging

Associations

To

Exploit

Service

Numerous employees did this during a changeover of ownership when management is still finding its feet and implementing some sort of procedures for smoother transactions? Whilst the new owner is yet to uncover the 'ugly truth' of what has been procured and concealed. Being fair to all concerned, I realised that we are all painting Banks with the same brush and I generally approach each situation with an understanding that both sides (there is always 3 sides to a story; yours, mine and the truth – wise words) played a role in the situation. The difficulty is that the Banker uses the Banks internal system so we are faced with a large organization protecting their internal operations and management rather than focusing on the ramifications of employee's actions. The best resolve is always a win/win because the Bank is the employer and is ultimately responsible for the business and their care of duty to the community. There is more at risk for them than just monetary compensation. Unless of course they are actually a Bad (Bank) Orchard owner, and they actually implemented the internal strategy to deceive customers?

> *Diva Tip: The code states that the bank does not have to provide a copy of your statements after 3 months … Watch OUT for this … Keep statements in a safe place!*

So if I were that Bad Apple, I would make certain that the worms within my sections were contained to avoid exposure.

For the Abuser of 'commercial' power, knowing that you are protected and having the ability to manipulate the internal systems make the temptations to obtain personal gain and gratification simple.

Having the Guidelines, policy, and procedure, not to mention the actual agreement (giving the bank all rights) that you execute under the bankers direction is a calculated plan, which allows the Bad Apple to get away with it. Temptation is a doable reality! God help those unsuspecting customers. These guys have the entire law behind them also. It's a no brainer and many have used the same techniques throughout their careers.

"Regardless that we are now MORE exposed to media stories of unconscionable actions of professional is still continues."

The reason for this comment is because of another matter; let's call the person Sam, who later realized the inconsistency relating to statements, indebtedness, documentation and the advices given by professionals.

Scenario: In Sam's matter it was really unclear as to the actual indebtedness that caused his Bankruptcy. On all the documents relied upon, most of the debts were repaid by the forced sale of assets. So, there was confusion and disbelief during this period. According to Sam and his documents there were many unanswered questions and all the while he was made to feel as though he had something to hide and had 'defaulted and caused these actions.

He didn't, he really had no idea how it all escalated to this extent. To his knowledge, he was able to work through the debt and offered a solution when 'his friendly banker' finally told him that his facility would not be renewed and had actually expired a few days prior! If he were allowed to sell his assets he would have received the entire amount and more. Sadly, he was not given this opportunity; so, when I reviewed his story, I too queried the indebtedness. The documents clearly revealed that he was capable of reaching a desired result for all parties.

*The statements were of a concern because I had the latest ones issued in 2014(a significant time after his bankruptcy); however, the ones relied on at appointment of a Receiver were nowhere to be found or sourced. **All is removed from Internet banking, even if you still have other accounts active**, that related account is nowhere to be found. So, I simply asked and, you guessed it, I couldn't get it! So, when the same question was asked of the Bank, (to their legal department) I was told to go back to the Statements! WOW. That is a catch 22, as they say. One minute I am told that my request for the statements was irrelevant, but they are relied heavily upon when it comes to an appointment of a*

Receiver or, worse, a Bankruptcy Notice.

It was strange that the indebtedness was not the first piece of information they had prepared for the mediation.

The confusion lies within the Code and regulations; the bank is supposed to assist you to work through issues. It cannot cause hardship, it must follow certain procedures, but doesn't. If the Bank has to show how it calculates interest and clarify changes made, then how does it explain having made a person Bankrupt without explanation of indebtedness? You'd think that would be simple, yet even after realising the outstanding debt, through sales they still claimed to have an outstanding facility? It then continued to bankrupt the customer for virtually the initial indebtedness? According to the statements, the debt was able to be worked through and was actually refinanced given the encumbrance was below the LVR (loan value ratio).

The Bank proceeded to exercise their rights under what could be classified as an unfair contract. (Given the explanation in the Legal journal) When asked to provide an explanation regarding the noted debt causing Bankruptcy the sad justification was finally provided as an 'internal formula' to do this type of calculation.

One used to calculate default interest after the fact; they had received their debt almost in full regardless of the discounted sale prices. The difference was minimal and was due to the added expenses of the disposal process.

So your Bad debt is incorporating a default interest regardless of the status and that simply means you are indebted to the bank until it decides to release you from Bankruptcy. A Bank can extend your bankruptcy if it so wishes, therefore you remain in their mercy.

So Beware, if your Bad Apple has the influence, you may never tell your story and get answers to a situation that is overwhelming from the onset.

The Code states that the Bank will:

Before **we** offer or give **you** a credit facility (or increase an existing credit facility), **we** will exercise the care and skill of a diligent and prudent banker in selecting and applying **our** credit assessment methods and in forming **our** opinion about **your** ability to repay it.

So the problem with this is that we rely on this prudent lending practice … we have no choice but to **'trust'**, you are great at what you do but you can't be expected to know everything. Now a

Banker is trained to provide you the best possible product for your situation, within the Bank's capacity as a lender. The Bank must always factor in the **risk** to both parties.

"THE PRUDENT LENDING REGULATIONS, ARE COMPROMISED BY THE BANK'S EMPLOYEES (BAD APPLES) AND THEY MANAGE TO GO UNPUNISHED. THE EMPLOYEE (BANKER) DOES NOT NEED TO HAVE AN AUSTRALIAN FINANCIAL SERVICES LICENSE (AFSL), IT IS NOT NECESSARY FOR A PERSON THAT IS REPRESENTING A LICENSEE."

So while you are going through the emotional ride of LIFE and obtaining financing for your dream home, a business venture, or you desperately must refinance, you would hope the banker will avoid placing you in a detrimental position. The banker knows very well the emotional state his customers are in and he knows how to induce emotions. We've all experienced it; I certainly have, especially when I was purchasing my very first home. To me it was not just a home, it was an enormous achievement personally and my banker knew this also. My Vulnerability was on display without me knowing it, but other could take advantage of.

"These days we are all trained in mindset, lead

generating, customer manipulation skills, and even cold calling is an art, to reach a certain stage in business or life. So, you are a target at all times regardless of how friendly your banker may be. he is not your partner in life or business."

The Code says: With **your** agreement, **we** will try to help **you** overcome **your** financial difficulties with any credit facility **you** have with **us**. **We** could, for example, work with **you** to develop a repayment plan. <u>If, at the time,</u> the <u>hardship variation provisions of the Uniform Consumer Credit Code</u> could apply to **your** circumstances; **we** will inform **you** about them.

So that is the catch phrase- (underlined) "*If at the time* and the *hardship provisions of Consumer Credit Code ... could apply*".

How would you know unless you were a banker perhaps? How many times has a banker freely offered Hardship provisions and mentioned various rights you have under the multitude of Codes and Practices. One of them is sure to suit your situation, but you may be quoted the ones that don't ... you just don't know. It is more common now but bankers hardly ever mentioned the Hardship clause, until the pressure was recently emphasized to do so. Now it is advertised distinctly on all websites. Probably so you can't say you did not know about it. The real issue is that you need to still be approved for it!

The problem lies with your Banker; whom has the ability placed you into a toxic facility to be able to have you removed inconspicuously. If they are a Bad Apple!

SCENARIO: Mandy had a home loan facility that was given to her whilst she was with her partner. At the time, she was requesting the loan be in her name only because she secretly feared that she would be declined and her partner would have to be included. Mandy broke up with her partner, who never actually helped with the mortgage, but did contribute to some of the living expenses. Mandy was demoted at work to a casual employee shortly after the breakup, so she went to her banker and asked for help. She was in despair and so emotionally worn out. The banker asked her to fill out an application for hardship and to wait for the department that handled this to contact her. A bit of time passed and she was rejected under some code and not meeting the criteria ... she explained this as I looked into her actual agreement. She was given a principal and interest loan, and when asked if she asked for this she said, "No."

Mandy specifically said to the banker that she would not be able to make the repayments. Although she was excited having been approved, she let her concerns be known to the banker. The friendly and eager banker, who was also a manager (not the big four), eased her concerns as she was guided to an office of an even friendlier professional she never met before, but was very close to this banker. Mandy said again that she could not meet her obligations if they were to be principal and interest, the banker stated that after the initial 12 months, he would have this reviewed and changed to interest only. The document was signed and the facility commenced.

Not long after Mandy notified the banker of the refusal, she asked if he would assist her to restructure the loan as he had promised. She received a notice of default and her file was moved to the head office of this bank. When we met, she was an emotional mess and she began to disclose her income capacity. The entire conversations she had with the various professionals, also with this new department at their head office needed to be reviewed. We submitted a complaint online to FOS (even if it did nothing, it bought Mandy time) **whilst there is an active complaint the Bank couldn't engage in debt collection activities.** *Then I helped her put an email together reiterating the conversations and events prior to her approval and upon execution of the documents.*

A request was made for a copy of the application; there was no response other than it will be sent to you shortly. I am sure this was to have its legal teams respond.

"Her matter was not dissimilar to my own previously and coincidently with the same Bank and same staff members!"

After a BS response stating the bank is within its rights, I contacted the banker on her behalf and requested a meeting.

During this meeting, we were able to show that various breeches were made and that Mandy never should have been approved according to her income capacity and situation. The banker was well aware of these facts and, although still refusing to show her the application, he did agree to review her file. Head office had to deal with the Ombudsman at this stage, a request for the application was asked of the Ombudsman, also. However, rather than waiting, I sent a detailed summation of events and requested that we have a mediated meeting because I was concerned that this matter fell within the boundaries of Maladministration.

It did and we managed to have her facility restructured into an interest-only loan that she could afford. Nine months from then, she had made repayments on time and decided to sell. Mandy paid back the bank and managed to make a profit on the sale, so she has purchased something smaller and has a better facility, one she is confident in repaying and still maintain a LIFE.

FOS came back with a conclusion that the Banks were well within their rights, so I suggested she request a copy of the file. The banks never supplied the completed application, no emails were provided, and a letter from that friendly professional stated that he advised her of the terms and conditions. (He never) The Banker claimed that there was no mention of interest-only after 12 months (another lie), so the ombudsman sided with the Bank.

It didn't matter ultimately because we had already resolved it and I guess the banker's report didn't make it quick enough to stop the complaint. I also did advise Mandy not to respond immediately; we sent a response eventually! Advising of the outcome and the ridiculous resolution of their office (FOS) considering the Bank had reached a decision. Although any type of settlement is done without admission, the suggestion was in their final actions.

There are many scenarios that clearly depict the act of non-support and no offering of Hardship. Again, there are so many Codes and legislation that even though you don't meet one of them, you may fall under another. It's hard to find the right resource when the directions are unclear.

Not being a Lawyer and doing it yourself can be a lot more favourable; you just need to understand how the systems work. Simple language, common sense and honesty works.

Tenacity and endurance helps too.

WHAT ABOUT BUSINESS-HARDSHIP MATTERS

Hardship and assistance should be provided as a compulsory practice you'd think. I would imagine that shareholders of every bank would rather a win/win situation over liquidation of assets...or do they?

During every Financial crisis, and we have seen a few I always believed and held the Banks responsible. (If only you could be a fly on the wall at their strategy meetings)Banks are allowed to create an appetite for an industry and lose their appetites just as quickly. There has to be a procedure in dealing with the Bad taste when they do.

Nicely speaking.

The Banks actions leave many unanswered and also

unasked questions when it comes to the rise and fall of many businesses.

During my adventures in Construction I have many scenarios and real life stories, both Good and Bad. However many involve the Bank's Bad Apples and also the friendly Administrators who all team up, especially where the assets are concerned.

SCENARIO: John had a development company that had completed a successful project, on time and under budget, with over 68% presold ... legitimately!

Remember, I came from the construction industry and I know all the games that are played. These sales were not to family, friends, neighbours, cats, and dogs. I have also helped banks when people have come to me claiming they were wronged when, in fact, the Bank's were on the receiving end of deceit. It is about fairness and the right thing. Working for Banks is one thing, working for people who have lost everything and were bankrupted is another all together.

So, John had been introduced to another banker by his previous banker. "A common practice perhaps, but in this case it was a Bad Apple who became a rotten Broker." This new banker has John pay a ridiculous establishment fee for a facility that was destined to fail within months of executing the document. It was more like the execution of his business and financial future! John's concerns were made clear to both the Broker and the Banker; however, he was reassured that the file would be personally managed and reviewed. It wasn't and no support was given to John. He was lead to believe that if he did not sign another agreement (Deed of Forbearance) that he would have a receiver placed on his business, even though he was managing his repayments?

John had proposed many various solutions for the bank to review and it was clear that if the bank did not want to cooperate and provide the support.

John's workout proposals would have paid back the indebtedness to the Bank and also a return for his business.

It was not accepted and no real explanation was provided.

When we asked for the response and review of the decision made by Asset Management Department, it would have made John cry.

You see John could have borrowed the short fall but because the banks were not willing to wait for the extra $80,000 shortfall.

*There was no rhythm or reason for the actions of the Bankers involved and although I classify these actions as part of the usual suspects, management chose to ignore the fact that their employees are conspiring against **customers of choice**.*

This was a sad matter given that John's home and that of family members were caught up in this securitization. He did everything to save it all and he could have. The bankers (broker) made money off this introduction and facility and the bank's response, along with the other regulators and lawyers who all stated that the banks were within their rights. There were avenues John could have taken to lead him to a favourable outcome but no one helped him.

John lost more than his business: he lost his family and he lost his dignity and, what is worse, it was not his doing.

He did the right thing and followed the rules.

He could not foresee the unethical motives behind the human being in power whom he trusted and relied on to act professionally.

> *Ugly Truth: It is difficult to dispute the actions of a Banker with the many facets surrounding our legal system and unless the Bank is prepared to listen without the shield of their legal guard dogs, nothing will change. All the actions described within this book have been resolved and the actual implications relating to the breech of many codes and policies were evident. Unfortunately no one listened or bothered to do any further investigations into the actually 'story' that would depict the actions of the Bad*

> *Apples and link them to the actual violation. The law was on the side of the banker and we were on the side of truth, tenacity and willingness.*

Sadly many had already endured the full force of the Bank's Rights and assistance of the Legal System that also takes away your voice and ability to be heard.

Banks need to realize that their Bad Apples create urgency, dependency and then a savior mentality amongst their customers.

- Urgency by delays in supposed credit approval process, creating a time constraint

- Dependency by becoming the only option available due to the first point

- Savior worship by promising to 'personally manage (Look after) the file and adding that all strings were pulled to 'get it over the line' all the while knowing the facility would cause difficulty

We become reliant on the advice provided by our banker however this relationship turns into more than a financial advice on the product and services. In John's case and many others the Banker is actually like a business adviser and the reliance becomes a dependency so you will usually follow that person like a loyal puppy dog, in search of assurance and security. That is how simple it is.

A Bank is not allowed to do as they do and train up their employees in a manner that allows them to follow internal protocol for dissolving facilities and at the same time increasing their personal quota with whomever they befriend and assist.

(Insider trading which is practically a daily occurrence- passing information to colleagues, assisting disqualified directors in setting up Phoenix companies and more)

The issue above is vast and has caused much heartache and pain for the innocent creditors who are defrauded by the Banks as well. The Banks may or may not be aware of these practices however it does not dispute the fact that there is so much more to implement and not simple change the wording of legislation and expect it to be solved or prevented.

"ABUSE IS ABUSE **NO** MATTER WHO INFLICTS IT OR HOW IT IS INFLICED"

The Code goes on and we continue to be frustrated.

<u>**We** will not accept **you** as a co-debtor under a credit facility where it is clear, on the facts known to **us**, that **you** will not receive any direct benefit under the facility</u>.

If only this were true in the case of many woman.

If a home is bought and the only person on the title is the husband, yet the loan had to be in both names, who has the benefit?

How does a bank determine if the co-debtor has benefits? What happens in a situation of Abuse and the wife has no choice; she cannot sell the home or force the sale. Her obligation is to the bank even though she may not have the financial benefits or control over her funds (if she has any). How do the banks monitor these loans?

In joint debts, what happens if the husband, who has been the provider, decides to stop paying and the facility goes into default? Does the bank offer assistance? No ... the bank's main concern is retrieving its debt and you generally become a number.

There are solutions and resources to protect you, depending on your situation. But everything is resolvable.

Guarantors

This is another Buyer Beware issue;

Signing as a guarantor even as a favour is a dangerous move unless you have a say in the daily activities of the main debtor ... in every situation... private or business!

SCENARIO: Rebecca was asked by her husband to sign as a guarantor for a piece of equipment his partner wanted. They had a small trucking business. So, reluctantly she did.

Mark didn't make the repayments on time and

Rebecca would receive demands to pay. Obviously it was Mark's responsibility, but the banks were content to accept payment from Rebecca and soon each time the facility was late Rebecca would get a call.

She became worried and when I insisted she request a payout because Mark had closed the company and vanished, she was unable to get one! Mark needed to make that request!

Many lengthy conversations were had, and I had pointed out the fact that the bank was willing to receive third-party payments, and we'd argue that they did not protect her from potential liability. They need to release the facility details to the guarantor to avoid having her name damaged, she held a very clean credit rating. That was important to her given her situation. This would have caused a domino effect to her business and reputation. What is really concerning in this matter was that the facility was introduced by a broker who received a fee, the guarantor had no idea of her obligations and the ramifications, and none of the said Code of Practices were adhered to.

As a guarantor, you are agreeing to take responsibility for the debt regardless that the Code of Practice suggests you can alter your limit of guarantee and all sorts of BS, which is never *usually done.*

*In all the cases I have assisted and my own experience, never have I seen anyone amend an agreement and for it to be accepted by the Bank. (I've tried, did it and when the Banks needed to reduce their long-term exposure, it was altered under their rights within the facility agreement) Guarantors have also lost everything in their names all because they signed a document that will usually secure **all your assets.***

> **Ugly Truth: The only way to remove your liability is to pay out the debtor's facility!**

That is stated as one of the options you have within the Code also!!

The code states that <u>if you are jointly and severally liable, we will allow you to terminate your liability</u> … then it continues with a contradiction. *<u>(Only if they can add the credit risk to the other party or someone else if you are lucky!)</u>*In reality, it is really hard to change the agreement or defend it after you have signed.

SCENARIO: In a matter where the woman suffered every form of Abuse by her controlling partner, she was pressured to sign the loan documents, however, had no other rights. It was a privilege for her name

177

to be on these papers, according to him. The banker was aware that things were not right in this relationship and continued to liaise only with the partner.

We'll call her Melinda for this purpose. After a horrific night of torment and non-visual abuse, Melinda had the strength to call the police. She was given her options and became even more terrified. She also discovered that her future really did depend on this man who was supposed to love her and respect her. If she did leave, the banks would pursue her for the debt if he stopped paying for the loan (she wasn't allowed to have money and he gave her an allowance).

Even if she did escape, he was able to ruin her financial future and get her into more problems; ones that leave you immobilized financially and appear to be your own doing from the outset. Where was she to go, and even by staying in the relationship she had no control or ability to protect herself? Melinda's fears were real and although many would say she had options, they were unknown and would be a battle regardless.

When you are mentally exhausted, any change into an unknown environment is unimaginable. She called the banker and asked to speak with him in confidence, since he assured her that it would be especially due to confidentiality requirements, she began by telling him that she had no ability to pay the loan and that she never understood what she was signing. "Could I be removed, please, as I cannot live like this?" Her words to him were at times muffled with tears.

The banker gave some lame response (Not worth repeating) almost scripted and said he would call her back.

That night Melinda ended up in the hospital.

The banker called the partner advising that these issues placed the loan in jeopardy AND MAY POTENTIALLY CAUSE A BREECH.

Ugly Truth: You must notify the Bank of any changes to circumstances and all needs to be approved by the Bank in writing. In some cases when it comes to change of Company officer holders, (that have been changed due to wrong doings of that person) these had been made with the assistance of a friendly banker and his associates. By allowing the regulations to be altered for some and not for other we are not on an equal playing field.

He should have lost his job but didn't … after putting the story together and submitting to the complaints department, nothing much was done. She finally escaped this relationship, the house was placed on the market, and all proceeds went to pay back the bank and the balance went to the partner. Melinda had to fight him legally for any of the proceeds; she didn't have the emotional or financial capacity to do so.

Trying to approach a banker is always a tricky task in this situation because the perpetrator is usually a completely different person to others and a monster to you. The banker, however, should have gone to his management in such a situation, but there was more to this story.

The relationship and the interaction between the banker and the partner were questionable to begin with, the mistake the Bad Apple had committed was that the document was signed without a witness (he did that later, without being present). Nothing was explained to Melinda, no terms and conditions were supplied, and the facility only benefited the partner and the banker (receiving the commission and perhaps a fee).

Melinda had a claim against the bank but had no energy and had no home, so rebuilding was the only priority. This was achieved without her having to relive the turmoil.

Besides my own experiences, this is the reason Diva Enterprises was born: to stop the inequality in LIFE. To eradicate the abuse that is perpetrated by many, it is not just behind closed doors. We have developed resources to help in the rebuilding of lives and to eliminate future abuse. There is so much a Bank can actually implement and not just for its employees, much needs to be done for customer confidence.

This scenario is only one of many that demonstrate how inconsistent the Code of Practice, Procedure and banking in general really is; these are guidelines and that is where the problems begin. How do you prevent a Bad Apple from infesting the others?

The problem is that we are dealing with Humans, not systems!

10. The Code will go into Advertising –

The problems we face should have no relevance to their advertising, apart for the fact it should not be misleading or deceptive. The fact is that Marketing and Advertising is to generate more business and we all have to do that. In all the real life scenarios, it would be easy to conclude that the advertising is misleading. **Buyer Beware is always the advice.**

All their products do not come with a satisfaction or product guarantee, no return or refund policy like other advertisers of products and services would have to provide. The Department of Fair-trading and the Consumer watchdog cannot do much in this space. Unfortunately, there is no mention of the truth behind *Debt Gone Wrong* and also how to manage your banker or how to detect a Bad Apple.

'Claims that you can and we will and it's possible to love a bank are all well created slogans, but unfortunately do not mean a thing legally.'

We are Listening…I don't think so given all the families that have been left to pick up the pieces as they watch the unfairness continue. Many Band aide solutions, campaigns and fee reductions that should have happened from the very beginning are now happening.

Many advertisements would have you believe that your bank is almost your partner in business, and in life to a certain degree. That is not exactly correct; the ugly truth is that many bankers go out of their way to befriend you and entice you to bank with them. That is all it is because once you sign, you give away your rights to anything really. It is against banking procedure for a banker to interfere with your finances, to give advice on daily running of a business, to make transfers without written instructions.

They are not your partners or friends as they quickly tell you during any dispute, complaint, or query into potential wrongdoing. I understand the saying; keep your friends close and your enemies closer, but the most realistic saying should be;

"Keep your friends close and your finances even closer"...MC

The banks have no reason to advertise these points. Do you really see them creating an ad say – **Deposit your cash with us, we promise to charge you for giving it to us!** Or,

WARNING: Deposit at own risk, as we may not give it back if we suffer a crisis like everywhere

else in the world!

Why not give your money to us – it's yours to use but belongs to us when you bank it into our business * Let's hope we don't fail you!

We promise to lend you money but will take everything you own when we feel like it!

We can make your dreams come true, even if you are overcommitted, and be confident we will be there to pick up the pieces and ensure your money is returned to us!

We are Lending (to anyone including directors still in liquidation deceiving creditors (including the Taxman) just ask one of our friendly Bad Apples. Or, go to our recommended Brokers (which we own) to help you make the not probable a reality at your own risk, until we get caught!

You found your dream home, let us help you create a nightmare … We know your house is overinflated, but we lend to the amount on the sales contract … no need to concern yourself with the real valuation!

Trust us, until we get caught out.

Our word is our promise and we welcome anyone to prove us wrong.

We hear you … until you sign our agreement, then we'll wish you luck all the way to court

We are focused on the future generation, making sure the debt culture continues to continue creating a better lifestyle (mainly ours)

Ok so that may not be fair or politically correct but it happens. You can prevent it, be responsible and don't be bullied and emotional manipulated. The Bank is there for a reason and it is a necessity, even with the new digital age just around the corner (now!). Regardless of the next best digital currency technique we need to also realize that when things go wrong we always have to revert back to basics. Then we rebuild and start again or simply because it was the easiest and best way. So we need institutions that are integrally operated and managed with humane ethics as the main priority. (We are not simply numbers on a balance sheet and we are responsible for a complete tribe)

Until this happens and people are made accountable for their actions remember you wouldn't give your life away stupidly treat your money the same way. Your financial future only has you to protect it from hard and according to the documents, only you to blame.… Not many will listen.

PART D: When it all goes south

The Code deals with - RESOLUTION OF DISPUTES, MONITORING, AND SANCTIONS

Code Compliance Monitoring Committee ("CCMC") comprising: The code tells us that the bank will have a committee made up of professionals who all have experience to determine who was in the wrong and if you have any rights.

'This is a frustrating process and the system, which was created centuries ago, is still based on the same fundamentals.' You borrowed the money, you signed the document, and you have to pay it back.

That is the simple truth and in the days where your Banker was as important as family we had no need to be as cautious. Corruption still went on but not as easily as now in my view. Now everyone is a target and before the rich and powerful were the targets. We have systems that allow ordinary battler to become potential victims of Greed.

It is so painstaking having to hear a professional tell you that the banker has met his obligations and has done nothing wrong ... as they sit blank faced and more concerned about making a BS (Badly supported) report that they have resolved another dispute. How do you dispute a banker's wrong doing with the bank, or any regulator whose survival depends on the BANK? **Meaning it is not**

in the interest of the Banks and their shareholders to expose the amount of infested fruit they continue to harvest.

Enquires continue to eat up taxpayer dollars and we cannot get a resolve much less an apology. The external regulators, even the media, have backed various stories and some of them are genuine and others didn't have completely clean hands. But, they were placed in a forum and made an example of. There are many stories that did not make this forum and it was because the customers did have clean hands and everyone got it, but didn't understand the complexities! That's because, the documents and the precise timing of the banker made it appear that there was no wrongdoing; in fact, it was the actions that weren't recorded that caused the problem. The factuality of the matter was clear; only the ability to excuse certain actions is where the frustration begins. Everyone could see the inconsistency with the facilities offered and the inherent potential breech that would leave the customer at the mercy of the banker. However the 'committee made up of professionals who all have experience to determine who was in the wrong and if you have any rights,' gave their opinion that was shown to be wrong! It is all too hard to actually investigate and it takes dedication and tenacity.

There is an underlining issue in the way the committees are formed and what they have achieved for individuals, and to be fair not many of them have lived or experienced this type of deceit.

Simply the problem is the punishment for the crime (and it is a crime) rather than simply giving Bad Apples more power than GOD. Sadly, God can't save you when there is no Justice, only injustice, in a well-versed system allowing Abuse to continue into another Orchard (BANK).

Until the **Law of Humanity** becomes a priority we are dependent on the one we have when dealing with Contract Law and Consumer Laws! All the Acts as well but the Act of Humanity is only considered in wars and actions concerning animal. The actions of the corrupt few (as the Banks would like us to believe) put fear and terror in the lives of many as their life becomes a battle ground and many live refugees in their own country.

We need be concerned about the unknown and unpredictable acts of terrorism, not about the person we have place trust.

Having dealt with some heartbreaking situations and getting results for people who no one who would listen to because of no funding, there is one final battle with a Goliath that is the biggest abuser.

We continue to allow all these actions to be wiped away with the same cloth that was established in the 1600s and perhaps earlier.

The stories (cases) where the victims all have clean hands would expose so much and open up a Pandora's Box, with only HOPE: to reform the entire system.

The enquiry has seen the Banks set up internal Customer advocates; I have to ask how many are bankers, or are they lawyers? If so, then do not speak without seeking out the same. Your words may be twisted and actions ignored because they are professionals and you're not. The Law is so broad and the terminology is confusing at the best of times. *(Investing in a dictionary dedicated to Legal Terms was the best $155.00dollars I had ever spent. No wonder lawyers have you pay up front, books are expensive when you want to understand our constitutional rights for justice)*

It's important to know with WHOM you are dealing with inside the walls of the Bank.

In one particular matter, the banker who was involved with another matter where he acted inappropriately was appointed as the customer advocacy specialist. Try getting past him to get to the CEO or someone responsible for the actions of its employees. That's not going to happen, so you cannot help but feel more disempowered and that feeling of Hopelessness as the banks continue to deflect accusations made within the forum of Question Time. Another enquiry silenced and another headline of "We Hear You" as the profits of many banks increases due to the ever-going Loan Book. Profits and dividends are dispersed and bonuses handed out as if it were Monopoly Money (illusionary currency), whilst you are left deflated once again and disillusioned with the entire world!

There are other issues when you face the 'specialised department of Asset Restructure" (CREDITMANAGEMENT), irrespective of the truth regarding the circumstances in your story, #**they don't care**.

Is it in its job description or in the Codes of We Don't Want Your Business Any More! The only document it cares about is the one that has now given it the ability to exercise its rights. So, whilst you look at the best way forward (the usual spiel), they are also looking at the best process and procedure (internally) to remove you. Meaning that there is a time frame for everything, not only the time restriction placed for you to raise complaint and request information.

So it is a well times and synchronized process.

There is a time frame in which a Bad Apple can appear to be **"generous in allowing you time"** because he is obligated to provide time to work through and assist you to come up with a proposal on how you will repay the debt. Sadly, he is also in control at all times. Ultimately he needs to approve any sales (*I've seen a bank delay a settlement many times or simply not show up!*), accept refinance or **not** (*under no obligation*), and basically be prepared to release its security. The choice is the banks and if you have signed a Deed of Forbearance, then you truly have no say. A Bad Apple can manipulate the story on your file, allowing another department to place the final nail on your coffin as he (and usually others within the system) places your financial future to Rest ... NO RIP *(Recourse for Inappropriate Procedures)*

After having the privilege of sharing many people's lives and stories relating to their experience with deeds, I likened it to being placed on life support temporarily, until the bank decided to pull the plug. Legally, it has the authority to do so and there is no recourse when it has killed the lives of innocent people. They do not face murder charges or manslaughter, for that matter.

During financial crisis, the fatality numbers increase, as many cannot face the pressure, frustration, depression, and feelings of failure and

191

defeat, having battled to justify and prove their credibility and integrity. For many, when all is lost and they have been stripped of their livelihood and dignity, not having the support and ability to seek justice for their loved ones, some see no way out.

You would think that if you had more equity in your property that the banks had no right to take action, wouldn't you? Well, they do and have! The documents are their license to do as they please regardless of the Human consequence, whatever is necessary for themselves in many ways and shareholders. There are many cases where this has occurred unjustly.

After all the recent enquiries, we have provided more power to ASIC, with the anticipation of a fair and just outcome. Many would argue that there are flaws in that process, as we have not yet witnessed management being held accountable for the damage its staff has instigated. Perhaps this is another example of the ability to manipulate the system and abuse many. This statement comes from the devastation left behind when rogue directors go into voluntary receivership knowing they can "get away" with the debts they created. They liquidate the company and start up, even become "shadow directors" for those who have deceived more than usual. The ATO are always at a loss, so technically it's taxpayers paying the price. Many of these situations involve the usual suspects with banking also and the issue of conflicted interest is camouflaged by the system.

ASIC has more than enough to do in regards to cleaning up their own internal systems and their handling of complaint, so how are they now going to handle the dealings of the Bad Apples that exists amongst their own organization?

Nothing is done, even with the enormous claims of fraud and injustice, against the employer who knowingly uses everything and everyone and purposely doesn't make payment toward statutory obligations. Employees and families lose out while the directors have built up a lifestyle that is based on ego and gluttony.

We continue to make complaints to ASIC in the hope that someone will hear us; however, even though the same person has had a multitude of complaints and proof of deception, nothing is done. If an ordinary director can get away with this, what is stopping the BANKS? Whilst the banks continue to announce the vast improvements they are implementing, we have not seen management or staff punished. Many are simply paid their salaries and entitlements and moved on.

Perhaps that is another way of saying they are anticipating that we'll allow them to draw a line in the sand and forget about the damage they've caused?

The manner in which many companies have failed their customers and employees in some cases is appalling. The directors have been allowed to manipulate the system and make a mockery out of the legislations. This is another story! The issue continues and it's no wonder so many people don't stand up or fight for their loss of livelihood. No one truly listens; they appease the situation whilst you're talking, then deny any wrongdoing. It continues as a vicious cycle.

We cannot continue to demand apologies from organizations that cannot and will not be able to correct the wrong doings of HUMAN BEINGS. We should insist that many are treated as criminals because it is fraud, theft and corrupt. The Laws need to apply to all and then perhaps a human being will think seriously before indulging in the temptation to enrich themselves or their associates.

It has to stop and we need to be focusing on living not searching for the truth and trying to uncover more corruption, every industry has done something wrong. Good Bad or Indifferent!

To stop Abuse we have to STOP and Take Responsibility of our lives and CHOICES...Do NOT allow anyone to take those choices away.

DON'T fall for the easy way out and be honest with yourself. We are the best person to know what we can and cannot afford.

The documents make you RESPONSIBLE and LIABLE so be that, don't blame anyone else for taking your financial future because you gave it away.

Harsh but practice...we cannot continue to fight the BANKS and waste more time that we will never get back. So to avoid this moving forward get all the tools you need and be confident with your finances. There are so many solutions and it all begins with you.

@Lipstick Strategies we will covers what to look out for and how to set up a honorable business life using the right makeup. It also provides the sunscreen so you don't get burnt. This is a gender-based metaphor because I believe that it must begin with females (No offence to any Males)

To avoid Abuse of any kind a girl needs to be financially abled and she must have a relationship with her money. No person should or can restrict you of that right. You need it to survive and to live and it should not change when you say I DO.

> *Choices are made from the HEART and not the HEAD...*

We are also a country with a large population of migrants these communities have settled in Austral and have mainly been self taught how to adapt and live by our Banking systems. No they are not the same as in most of their countries. The general terms of savings and borrow money you pay it back is the main thought process however there is so much for many to yet discover.

We need to include the females of these settlers to empower them also and avoid any uninvited abuse.

Many of the people in these cases are Men and I have always been in Male dominated industries so it works for all. My mission is to educate girls so that they do not go into LIFE with only the knowledge imparted by the obvious teachers. There is so much to understand about things we claim to know. If one person goes away with a seed of possibility that may sprout when she is faced in an unpredictable and impossible situation then we've changed a life.

Having someone in the family able to have the resources and calmness in difficulties and in general daily events helps that entire families future.

Men are great and they are still generally boys and have egos and tend to keep it all in but do crumble and some face the fear in a different way. A treat is a threat and we all come out fighting in different ways, however when one of you is able to CALM the situation down it makes for a better result.

Ultimately it is about avoiding these scenarios all together but having the ability if it does occur, to protect yourself.

So what are we to do now?

Rather than write an entire encyclopedia, we decided to write a smaller series of programs and blueprints that will explain certain documents, situations, and resources that have been proven to undo what's been done, but also prepare you for what could happen. Allowing you to ride the wave during the storm because the orchard (Banking) will always survive as history has shown us.

If the tsunami didn't rid the Orchard of its infested crop through these years, where so much had been exposed, then we can be confident that the rot will spread. At least until one day human nature will be more compassionate and realise that the customer across the table is also a human and not a money sign.

$$$$$$$$$$

History repeating but not hurting as much; **Is it a Lie or a repeat of ignorance?**

Having reviewed many books and papers relating to various subjects: banking, economics, currency, money (yes it is considered different), real estate, laws and regulations, and more, let me tell you it is confusing at the best of times understanding the different styles of explanation. Simply put, people lie and history repeats and we are still unable to foresee the probabilities of the same occurrence.

"The further backward you look, the further forward you are likely to see" ... Winston Churchill

My God ... I said after reading somewhere that the first currency crash happened in Greece. To my entire community of Greek friends, I had to admit that it appeared everything came from the Greeks! (Jokingly)

But in all seriousness, it happened in 407 BC when the currency was gold and silver, a tangible asset. Gold and Silver have been around as the main form of currency for 4,500 years, so it developed from there. Then it became minted into coins of equal weight, during this time Athens became the world's first democracy ... so you can blame them for taxes, also!

Then the inevitable happened, the great civilisation that it was fell; as history goes, this is caused by irresponsible lending (greed) and war! The Greeks then discovered a clever way to use the coins they received in taxes, mixed another metal, and created double the amount for nothing! Deficits were created ... the government created its own money.

Greece crashes and the Romans take over and attempt to perfect the term "currency" (Money was tangible and made sense even with the barter systems that were used). The Romans did as the Greeks and substituted the gold with other metals, but now they created revaluation. The same coins but a different face value, the government also dictated for how much a merchant could sell his goods, so with no profits to be made, they had to shut shop, either find work or they went on welfare.

The Dole came out of Rome! (You must remember I never studied History, so I'm keeping it light, although I have made up for it now!) Anyway back to history ... in Rome they faced giving out free wheat to a high percentage on welfare, so the government employed more soldiers (work for the Dole) and invested in Projects (Public Works, infrastructure, etc ...) spending more money than they had. They then ran out of money, so they made more by using bronze and copper, corrupting currency, as I call it! Some say this was the demise of the Roman Empire, yet they concurred with the illusion of a healthy economy based on a money-making scheme (my interpretation only – for all the history buffs out there)

As I continue reading the various versions, I finally decided that we have not really formed new legislations, but simply modified what has been done for centuries. Yet we do not learn, as the people who govern have not lived the lives of many ordinary individuals. (Very rarely)

Paper money came into play and in all I have read it continues without ramification to those in power, but the damage this is causing to people's lives is another issue that has played out for centuries, also. Reading about John Law and banking was another "really, how?" moment. He was given a bank and allowed to print paper currency. Even Wikipedia states he was a gambler and because of his friendship with a person of power was allowed to do this (maybe he was the only man for the job!). However, being an extraordinary mathematician, he became the wealthiest and most powerful financial figure in the whole of Europe. He was given a business (Bank in the USA) for which he decided to sell shares to the trusting public, he had the confidence of the public and that exploded, becoming the even more powerful. Law's bank, the Banque Royale was basically the central bank of France. He now had the Government backing his paper notes, allowing the issue of more notes and this allowed more spending. If the people want money, they shall have it mentality. Somehow I don't think people consider the consequences of greed.

Going through the journals and papers, a pattern is clearly seen: if this paper money just paid off the country/s debt, it meant we can spend more … all they had to do was print more notes.

When things are going good, why would anyone consider it going bad?

In 1720, France went through it own crisis, after all the prosperity, inflation, housing skyrocketing, and daily living expenses rising, it came to a head when notes were cashed in for gold. That year the bank closed, the collapse saw France and other parts of Europe fall into a terrible depression. Could that happen to us here, housing is so far out of reach, incomes have not risen to cover standard living costs and we are constantly selling of our countries assets to improve economy (paying for infrastructure)? Is that what it means?

It appears that during the times of war, more notes were printed. How and why does not make sense to me after all the reading I did, so I asked an old relative who served in the German Army and he explained it simply. "Power, Ego and Greed." In Germany, at least at one time Marks (its money) were being printed to show that the country was able to survive. A country was overruled if it could not pay back to its neighbouring countries the debt incurred. Law of the Land, really, but whose laws were they?

Basically, this is a cycle that has lasted throughout the centuries and it continues without much change; however, consequences may have. If we look at the United States (which we do most of the time), it developed the first National Monetary Commission in 1908 after the issues with banks in 1907 suspected of causing the crashes (demise) then foreclosing and selling assets at a profit. This sounds very similar to practices still done in today's bank procedures, especially with the receiverships process.

Now this Commission was to investigate the head of each bank involved, they were also considered the wealthiest of men. What happened next was how it appears in the current climate in banking and the regulators. It is reported the Senator invited all of the people involved for a secret meeting of sorts; to come up with an outcome to satisfy the public and impose a better regulated system. The same men accused of the manipulation and misconduct were the same men to create the Federal Reserve in America. So we do actually follow America according to history, or is it the best practices from all over the world. If this is the case, why are we not observing and learning from the mistakes and the patterns of the economic cycles? I guess we are following.

We felt the GFC, however, not as badly as other parts of the world; many suffered at the hands of those in a more powerful position because you become vulnerable when the Bank decides it no longer wants your debt risk. Sometimes the Banks were in the right and there are many people who set up businesses (projects) and misused the funds. Others have also deceived the banks into providing excessive funds. That happens, also, but there are far more who were caught in the crossfire of management directives without warning. Some of our Banks with parent companies in other parts of the world made it easier for Australian banks to acquire them during the GFC. For some it was a prosperous environment, and for many it was despair.

The problem is, and has always been, that the Bank is in the best position to foresee such actions, but also the instigator and navigator of Booms and Crashes. A bank has the ability to create a false economy with the writing of loans, usually a loan book and I often wonder with the almost trillion-dollar debt in our country how on earth are we to survive? If the Bank has to keep 20% of all deposited funds as available reserves, does it lend out 80%? Or, does it mean 100% of the depositors' money is in the bank and the bank creates the additional 80% in new currency through its loan book ... they have an asset and other security if necessary, right?

So how does it work when our governments borrow the Reserve Banks' funds?

Is it the same as the USA? The Reserve banks prints more money when it is needed and as we (government) pay back the principle debt, we borrow more to pay the interest?

In the United States it appeared much more simple than here in Australia; my cousin elaborates that it is different when you live there. It isn't easy because you have to declare yourself bankrupt and hand back the keys to your home when you cannot pay the mortgage. WOW!

In Australia, we are a complex bunch, we not only borrow money to buy our homes, we never actually own them. We have a loan with the bank regardless of how we obtain this loan and as soon as there is a change internally for the lender and you cannot pay the interest, you are defaulted, sold up, bankrupted, along with everyone else who is involved with you within that facility. We witnessed the property boom and also the crash of 2007-2010; as we reach that seven year itch, are we prepared for what is likely to happen? It seems to be at the 10 year point it all turns to SHIT…and no amount of air freshener will rid the stench of despair.

Where can we go from here, as many are finding it more and more difficult to survive daily, much less affordably, after rushing to get into a debt because "interest rates are at all-time lows"?

If we are reliant on the Banks to be responsible in their lending practices, I wonder who's fault will it be when, not if, prices stabilise or fall slightly or the banks' need to increase interest to sustain the debt to capital ratio. The debt becomes unmanageable because your sale price was already $400,000 above market price. Now your home is not valued in the same manner and you cannot rely on the previous valuation that showed the value as per the sale contract price. After all, these years I am certain the banks would realise the true value is not the sale price, but usually the detail in the bank's valuation that you do not see. However, since 2014-15 and on, the banks have been borrowing over 100% LVR if we consider general lending practices.

If the house I purchased for $1 million (a cheap price in Sydney) and its true value is $680,000.00, the bank gave me a loan of $900,000 in 2015. My mortgage and living expenses are already causing a burden, even at a low interest. Who will have the rights when the interest increase and the values shift?

Will you have a leg to stand on?

The example above is only a minor one; so many facilities were already signed up prior to the banks' lending reforms so people were being approved like it was free funds! Now many are already feeling the pressure because they were availed of a facility that would surely destroy them in the future.

Before the tighter lending reform and risk assessment (now maintenance strategy) brokers and bankers were repeating the actions of 2007 ... just before the GFC. It is also happening in the business sector; In 2015, a few banks even leant enormous funds to directors of companies in liquidation (yet to be liquidated!), then when more complaints were made to ASIC and the bank shadow directors replaced the person and their lives continue as so many others had theirs destroyed. It's whom you know and the Bad Apples know each other, so they assist those they see fit! Until they have to throw each other under a BUS! These activities also hurt the bank to a small degree, but not as much as the frustrated and innocent families left to continue battling.

Banking facilities destine to fail won't hurt the bank as much as it will hurt you. There are things you can do to protect yourself and your family.

It is sad to think that the banks have been negligent in their lending practices all due to revenue raising and greed, but they are a business at the end of the day. As we continue the many enquiries and quest for Royal Commissions, you should be looking at resources to protect your assets early because the bank is well aware of its cycles and has not helped the situation.

We continue to argue with the system when ultimately it is the Human behind the computer screen who has the power to manipulate the system and abuse his position in a Banking culture that began with clever males.

It needs to go Beyond the Men of the past who set the patterns of behaviour.

Nothing much has really changed the cycle of abuse, manipulation, and corruption that continues whilst the solutions have all remained the same.

So, now we introduce Banking Beyond Men to educate into a better Money Management for LIFE.

After a team effort with other extraordinary, disruptively talented women, we will give back voices to many who have been abused by a system that was initially designed for the creation of civilisation and not the destruction of lives.

Financial Planning with a difference and Advocacy skills made available through our seminars that will create change. Teaching you what others do not want you to know. Avoiding the nightmare of Financial Frustration. Learning that financial responsibility leads to Freedom and Fun. Having Choices in all aspects of your L.I.F.E

Financial Diva – Sacha Burchgart: Who is she? She is a woman that was tired of the competing and lack of respect, equality and ultimately fairness within the industry. Sacha is first and foremost an ordinary woman who has faced challenges and dealt with LIFE the only way she knew how ... Good, Bad, or

Indifferent, but she was compassionate, honest, and loyal. A devoted wife and mother, Sacha holds her Diploma of Financial Planning. She is a certified Self-Managed Superannuation Fund Adviser, a member of the Association of Financial Planners (AFA), and the Self-Managed Superannuation Fund Association (SMSFA). She currently sits on the Affinia Adviser Council and has won the Affinia Chairman's award in 2015 and the Affinia Practice of Year in 2016.

International Diva of India: Bhavini Mehta

Bhavini has been on this journey for change with me and has encouraged me to continue when it became too exhaustive and personally draining. She is a wealth of knowledge and has so much resilience, compassion, and determination. A wife and mother first and foremost with the desire to Create a future of which her daughter can be proud, she will educate and empower the women of India as all need to be aware of their rights and responsibilities to themselves ultimately.

In Australia, the Indian community is very prominent and whilst it endeavors to understand and accept the cultures of our country they, too, need to be aware of the Bad Apples. Bhavini will see to this.

There are so many people to thank in our lives and,

in this case, I thank the voiceless victims who had placed their trust in me. I am honoured to say we are friends in LIFE as the journey has been an emotional rollercoaster for everyone involved.

Never forget where you came from and never stop believing in your truth, no matter how ugly others have made it into.

KEEPING THEM HONEST

Do You know what it is costing Tax Payers to keep these mammoth corporations in the Banking Industry 'Honest' and what it can potentially cost the Government?

That is a question I dare not answer and truly no one would ever know, who is able to calculate the amount already spent on enquiries and also what if 'the Royal Commission' did eventuate, who would bail out the Bank's Business?

Investigations and Audits

Internal or external what is the difference?

Internally it would appear biased (one-sided) some could think that it would allow a cover up and that defeats the purpose. How does an external audit benefit uncovering the truth when a GIANT organisation such as a Bank, when it is employed by them?

An external party to do this at arm's length is near impossible? Within the circle of Finance everyone knows everyone and the Banking dynasty, provides a lot of work to many professional bodies and also funds their lifestyles. Meaning everyone is practically indebted to a Bank!

Having now sat through years of enquiries observing question times, I can't help by giggle through some of the lame questions and answers especially. It's almost like being called to the principal's office and answering the questions (accusations supposedly) and knowing you may get the cane, The laws and regulations are so lenient now that you only get a lecture and the idle threats of potential action.

Internal audits have to be done for a publicly listed business that benefits the shareholders mainly, they do not have to complete an Audit but must prepare and provide financial statements to inform the public. As the 'Public' we are aware the Banks are continuing to make enormous profits whilst many Bank employees get away with Abuse of Position and are rewarded by these profits.

How do these audits detect the actions of fraud, misleading conduct and maladministration by their employees? It is much easier to cover up these actions given the magnitude of the business and the system that is based on a one size fits all model, however it is hard to keep people honest and responsible for their action. To commit an act of Fraud i.e.; intentional deception with the view to gaining personal advantage, by misleading customers into facilities they cannot service (for internal gain and incentives as an example), hiding or manipulating transaction and more is readily committed in Banks. Why, because they have a greater chance of success and no detection as they usually either move onto another Bank or work their way up to management status.

The employer would have to investigate every transaction and that would be near impossible given the size of any Bank, not to mention that any activity that is undertaken and that takes the management away from daily duties are charged back to the customer in some way.

As explained in the earlier chapters their business model in one based on customers funds really.

Then we have the 'Errors' i.e.; a result of unintentional mistakes like when a bank has accidently entered in a date and you receive millions of dollars into your account. The interest that has increased but not easily detected (I rarely checked my statements and just allowed the direct debits to continue, never paying attention to any changes that may or may not have occurred), fees charged but not warranted.

Any Audit will provide a 'reasonable assurance' that there are no errors in the statement, it does not guarantee that there are NO errors.

Any of the Figures Professionals- Accountants or Auditors provide a personal guarantee because they will be held accountable for another human's actions. A good example is a colourful accountant can get away with doing the wrong thing because you sign a waiver that states he relied on the information 'YOU' provided. The Banker Auditors would or should be doing the same.

Opinions and Conclusions arising from Audits.

The various results of an audit can usually be broken down into 3 modifications based on their findings, qualifications, adverse or disclaimer opinions. These are generally issued because of; *Disagreement*; generally accepting accounting. *Uncertainty* is an inability to obtain appropriate evidence. Adverse; this is Bad! Meaning there was no evidence the financial statements are not true and fair...but hardly happens to a Bank. *It does happen to ordinary businesses that Banks audit for further or future funding. So how do we expect a Royal Commission to be played out?*

Will it become a lengthy and costly exercise only to discover that there are no findings that can be persecuted or reformed? Or will it be a costly and timely exercise to draw a line in the sand when everyone discovers that to hold each and every perpetrator accountable will cause a significant collapse of the Banking Industry? Who and how will it play out or should we turn to the rest of the Globe and quickly discover how to protect our country and not make the same mistakes.

The first step is to STOP and take responsibility of our Financial Future, protect it like you would the life of your loved one and more importantly yourself.

If you become self aware and savvy (Boy's remove the EGO) you will always stay one step ahead of anyone with ulterior motives.

The Bank as an employer cannot control each and every member of staff but they should be accountable for their ethics and manner when dealing with issues raised and not just pass it on to someone else to handle whilst accepting exorbitant salaries for their ability to create more wealth for shareholders who have no real concept of the daily dealings.

We are actually fighting 'Human Nature' something that no one can control and behavioral laws have not figured out to date.

How do you STOP a person from abusing anything?

In short: The Banking system is one that has provided internal procedures and policies to protect their risk exposure. The problem is same system has been used for the personal gain of humans in a position of power and not for the intended purpose. Therefore this has and will continue causing the Banks to investigate and alter their wording to suit. A system that warns the bank of Risk adverse facilities that have a potential of collapse for example. The issue is that the person operating the keyboard to enter data, can manipulate the situation and use that same systems to 'remove' a customer at will, making it seem as though they were a Bad Banking Risk.

These systems or structures allow the bank to improve their Risk Management (or whatever name given) to remove or wind down loans through strategic structures providing advantages such as lower capital and funding requirements. These however can be constructed and implemented easily by a professional that knows and understands how to manipulate the system to appear to be performing his duties and obligations as an employee. The problem here is that these actions don't necessarily help the Bank. The benefits lie with the Banker and his associates (third party benefactors) who usually gain an asset or monetary remuneration.

The Banks are only the service vehicle used to Abuse many unsuspecting customers and there is no discrimination here everyone is treated equally for a CHANGE!

It is time to get REAL and FAIR in a world that is fighting the possibility of Unknown and Undetected Terror, we DO NOT need to be fearful of trusting Banks too.

PART E:

Definitions as explained by the Code of Practice and my own personal acronyms.

In this **Code,** any words in bold, **like this,** have the following meanings:

ABA: means the Australian Bankers' Association.

ASIC: means the Australian Securities and Investments Commission.

Australia: includes New South Wales, Queensland, Victoria, Northern Territory, South Australia, and Western Australia

Bank: means a business approved by law to carry on the general business of funding/banking in **Australia** that is authorised under the Banking Act 1959 (history) to use the word "bank" or a similar expression in its name.

Orchard: *A plantation from where a particular harvest is generated.*

Banking service: means any financial service or product provided by **banks** in **Australia** to **you**: **the Public**

Bad Apple: An Employee of the Bank that acts

GFC: does not mean Global Financial Crisis for me it actually stands for General Finance Culture

CV: does not mean Curriculum Vitae it to me stands for **Certified victimization.**

Goliath: The Banks

Pesticides: Regulatory bodies